RASPBERRIES AND RHUBARBS

CONVERSATIONS & SITUATIONS BY
KATHARINE MILLER

Published by
Sparkling Observationalist
sparklingobservationalist.com
thatkatharine.com

©2020 Sparkling Observationalist, Katharine!
All rights reserved.
03 15 20 4 3 2 1

No part of this book may be performed or reproduced in any form without written permission from the author and publisher, except in the context of reviews.

This is a work of fiction. Names, characters, businesses, places, events, locales, and incidents are either the products of the author's imagination or used in a fictitious manner. Any resemblance to actual persons, living or dead, or actual events is purely coincidental.

ISBN: 978-0-9919031-5-3

Miller, Katharine, 1979–
Raspberries and rhubarbs / Katharine Miller.

SCENES

AU REVOIR, RESERVOIR RENDEZVOUS 9
six characters (6M)
A group of conmen wait to perform a heist.

BODY IN THE LIBRARY 18
characters (5X, 7F, 12M)
A cast of dozens marvel over a body being found in a manor's library.

CAR TROUBLE 23
two characters (1F, 1M)
A mid-40s suburban couple encounter potential delays en route to their first official date.

THE CONSULTATION 33
two characters (2M)
A nebbish man in the midst of a life crisis seeks guidance from a tattoo artist to make a lasting impression.

DEEP CUTS 43
two characters (1F, 1M)
A couple attempts to disconnect and reconnect on a weekend getaway.

EINE KLEINE FAHRSTUHLMUSIK 54
two characters (1F, 1M)
The eternal struggle to bring art and entertainment to the general public has a building manager at odds with a piano player.

EVERYTHING MUST GO 60
three characters (1F, 2M)
Two mannequins plot their escape from a closing department store.

FRANKENSTEIN'S FRIAR 70
one character (1M)
Frankenstein's creature performs a stand-up routine.

GRANDPA GIRLFRIEND   72
two characters (1F, 1M)
A couple discusses a development that could impact their relationship.

THE HEIRESS' HABIT   77
two characters (1F, 1M)
Katharine Drexel, heiress to the Drexel fortune and aspiring nun, discusses her vocation with her trusted advisor, Bishop James O'Connor. (historical fiction)

INCESTRY DOT COM   89
two characters (2F)
A mother and daughter discuss their family history in the Deep South.

THE LEGEND OF S   95
one character (1M)
A manic professor delivers a lecture on the origin of a mysterious symbol.

MILESTONES   100
three characters (1F, 2M)
Harry's in for a big birthday surprise when he finds his wife and best friend in bed together.

MYSTERY SOLVED   110
one character (1M)
Lord Roland Butterfield-Jones solves a most pressing mystery in Hrmsforth Manor.

PHILOSOPHR 2.0   113
one character (any)
A millennial philosopher recounts a litany of nonsensical calamities.

POPPYCOCK RISING   116
three characters (3X)
A lighthearted look at the struggles that writers face in the modern gig economy.

AU REVOIR, RESERVOIR RENDEZVOUS

A group of conmen wait to perform a heist.

CAST:
MR. BLISTER-PACK - *naive, eager*
MR. BUTTERSCOTCH - *mouthy, sarcastic*
MR. ZIPPO - *mature, implied leader of the group*
MR. WET WIPE - *silent, intimidating*
MR. STALE FRY - *milquetoast, nervous*
MR. SLURPEE - *easily provoked, old-fashioned*

SETTING: *An abandoned warehouse in a derelict industrial area*

Six guys are sitting around the abandoned warehouse.

STALE FRY: So, they were showing that old movie Sergeant York on TV last night and it got me thinking, you know how Bewitched had those two Darrins? Remember? The first Darrin was Dick York and then he was replaced by Dick Sargent with no explanation. I mean, not even a magical "Endora cast a spell on Derwood" kind of reason. Weird, right?

ZIPPO: What's that got to do with the movie?

STALE FRY: It's got nothin' to do with the movie.

ZIPPO: Then what's your point?

STALE FRY: It's funny, y'know.

ZIPPO: No. I don't know. If you're trying to make a connection between a 1940s war movie and a 1960s situation comedy, you're not finding it, my friend.

STALE FRY: Oh. Well. I thought the name thing, y'know, was it coincidence? Did they cast it that way on purpose? What're the odds, right?

SLURPEE: You got internet on that phone of yours?

STALE FRY: Yeah.

SLURPEE: Why don't you look it up on www dot nobody gives a fuck dot com?

BLISTER-PACK: Guys, what're we doing here?

ZIPPO: Waitin' to hear from the boss.

BLISTER-PACK: But why do they — *(gestures to audience)* — need to see this?

ZIPPO: You don't know what you're talking about.

BUTTERSCOTCH: It's probably supposed to give 'em a sense of who are, so maybe they're sad or somethin' if one of us gets gunned down.

SLURPEE: Who's gettin' gunned down?!

BUTTERSCOTCH: Somebody. Maybe nobody. We don't know yet. I mean, odds are at least one guy'll be taken out. You ever been on a job where at least one guy didn't make it? So, you gotta figure, we're gonna lose a guy. Probably that guy in the back, he ain't said much. Although, maybe he's part of a big twist at the end, so it makes sense that he's all quiet and mysterious now. Or maybe he's got a comically high voice that undermines his intimidating figure. Is that it, guy? You got a Mickey Mouse squeak over there? A Porky p-p-Pig stutter? Whassa matter, puddy tat got your tongue there, Grape Ape?

WET WIPE scowls silently at BUTTERSCOTCH.

SLURPEE: You got a lotta maybes for a big talker, Butterscotch.

BUTTERSCOTCH: What does that mean?

SLURPEE: You know what it means.

STALE FRY: C'mon, we're just sittin' around here talkin'.

BLISTER-PACK: Exactly. Who wants to see that? We're just wasting time. Let's cut to the action, already!

ZIPPO: Look, we're here and we stay put until the boss says it's go time.

BLISTER-PACK: What if he doesn't call?

ZIPPO: The boss'll call.

BLISTER-PACK: But what if he doesn't?

STALE FRY: Why're you so sure the boss is a man? None of us met 'em before, right?

SLURPEE: The boss is a man alright.

BUTTERSCOTCH: You're so sure?

SLURPEE: 'Course I'm sure. Ain't no dame capable of planning a heist this complex.

BUTTERSCOTCH: You ain't spent too much time with dames then.

SLURPEE: I spend enough time with 'em, you know what I'm sayin'.

BUTTERSCOTCH: That's not what I heard.

SLURPEE: Who you gonna believe, your ears or my fists?

SLURPEE and BUTTERSCOTCH lunge at each other. ZIPPO steps in and motions for them to settle down. SLURPEE and BUTTERSCOTCH back off.

STALE FRY: What if there ain't no heist?

ZIPPO: We know there's a heist.

STALE FRY: Yeah, I mean, we know there's supposed to be a heist but what if they — *(gestures to audience)* — get just two hours of us shooting the shit in this warehouse? There's all this build up and no actual heist.

ZIPPO: Nobody's seeing nothing here.

BUTTERSCOTCH: What if we manufacture some tension amongst ourselves — start arguing over who gets the bigger cut, maybe discover hidden connections between certain guys. Hey, Zippo, weren't you hot and heavy at one time with Slurpee's dame… what was her name… Ditsy? Mitzi?

SLURPEE: What?! Lemme at him—

SLURPEE lunges at ZIPPO, but STALE FRY intervenes and settles him.

BLISTER-PACK: Nah. We gotta see the heist. There's too much potential for excitement — who gets in, who gets out? How do we pull it off? What's at stake? Does something explode? All that makes a way better movie than a buncha joes yammering at each other.

BUTTERSCOTCH: Maybe there's no budget for action sequences but they could afford a half dozen out-of-work schlubs to sit around gabbing like housewives. Maybe the actual heist is bilking these folks out of their hard-earned cash by making them think they're getting quality entertainment when they're really gettin' a lotta garbage written by somebody who's been wearing the same pajamas for a week and a half.

SLURPEE: There you go with the maybes again.

BLISTER-PACK: Alright, so, if we ain't gonna show the heist, how're they gonna know what happened? Do we come back here after and high-five or what?

ZIPPO: That's not part of the plan.

BLISTER-PACK: The plan was to rendezvous here to wait for the signal, do the heist, then split up and lay low until things cool off. But dontcha think they'll be curious how it turns out?

BUTTERSCOTCH: Tell you what — after we pull the heist and split up, I'll come back here and do a play-by-play sum-up, alright?

ZIPPO: If we could, please refrain from breaking the fourth wall, fellas. It's there for a reason. Let's go over the plan again.

Guys mutter in agreement. They pause, think, look puzzled.

ZIPPO: You fellas know the plan, right?

STALE FRY: I knew it! There's no heist!

BUTTERSCOTCH: We've been over it before.

SLURPEE: Yeah, we were here and some guy in a velour jumpsuit mumbled a buncha stuff at us… somethin' about a royal chick's bust, a baseball sapphire, and lugging out some dame in an Oriental carpet?

BLISTER-PACK: And we got our names — *(points to himself, then each character as he names them)* Mr. Blister-Pack, Mr. Zippo, Mr. Slurpee, Mr. Stale Fry, Mr. Wet Wipe, and Mr. Butterscotch.

STALE FRY: Anybody else bothered that our names all sound like junk you find between the car seats?

BUTTERSCOTCH: We're definitely not gettin' into that again.

BLISTER-PACK: Anyone else curious why the boss ain't playing a bigger part in the heist? We did all the planning, the plotting, the stuff with binoculars and blueprints and they ain't shown up once to supervise or nothing. Here we are putting our lives on the line, for what? A few lousy bucks and getting our wounds tended to by an unscrupulous veterinarian? We should get together and demand better treatment.

BUTTERSCOTCH: I told ya before, Blister-Pack, you can't unionize criminals.

BLISTER-PACK: What about the Mafia? They're organized.

STALE FRY: How do we know the boss ain't here?

Guys groan.

BUTTERSCOTCH: I suppose you think the mastermind of our operation is masquerading as part of our ragtag gang with the intention of pitting us against each other so we kill each other and he can get away with all the loot? My money's on Wet Wipe over there. Hey, Marcel Marceau, you wanna chime in here?

WET WIPE moves to launch into a speech but is interrupted by ZIPPO.

ZIPPO: Enough! Questions comin' into this ear, questions goin' outta that ear. Are we in a movie or in a play? Is there a heist or isn't there? Is the boss a broad or ain't she? I don't know. All I know is I was hired to do a job and now I'm listening to a buncha buffoons babblin' on with "they were showing a movie" and "oh, what if they don't see us pulling the heist." You got us surrounded by "theys" when you should be worried about being surrounded by cops. We don't need an audience to pull the kinda job we're about to pull. Now, could you all just focus on your own tasks while we wait for the boss to call?

The guys sit in silence for half a beat.

STALE FRY: Hey, how come there ain't no broads in this scene?

SLURPEE: Look, you wanna see a buncha broads pulling a heist, go write it yourself. This is a buncha men pulling a heist.

BLISTER-PACK: Or a buncha men talking about pulling a heist.

STALE FRY: I don't think a guy should write a movie about women doing anything. Whadda guys know about the female psyche and whatnot?

SLURPEE: Women know jack squat about men but they got no problem writin' us like a buncha useless pansies.

BUTTERSCOTCH: Y'know, men and women ain't so different as we're taught to think. We could all be replaced by chicks here and it wouldn't make no difference. A dame could crack a safe as well as me. If I recall, Mitzi was a great getaway car driver.

SLURPEE: Don't go talkin' 'bout my Mitzi. If I catch her name outta your mouth again—

BLISTER-PACK: It was a compliment, man.

SLURPEE: Yeah, well. Don't matter. My Mitzi ain't no getaway driver no more. She's gonna be respectable.

ZIPPO: Ha! Best of luck to ya, pal. May you succeed where we all failed.

SLURPEE: What? You all know Mitzi?

Guys laugh.

ZIPPO: Every two-bit conman from here to Tijuana knows Mitzi.

BLISTER-PACK: Mitzi gave me my first job.

ZIPPO: Mitzi gave me a lotta good times.

STALE FRY: Mitzi gave me chlamydia.

SLURPEE: She ain't like that no more. After this job, she and I are giving up the cons and going straight.

Guys laugh harder. SLURPEE can't decide who to hit first, so he punches a table and flops onto a chair to sulk.

ZIPPO: *(checks his phone)* We should've heard something by now.

BLISTER-PACK: What do we do?

ZIPPO: Stay here and wait.

BLISTER-PACK: This is getting dull. We gotta get out of this room.

BUTTERSCOTCH: We've only been here ten minutes.

STALE FRY: Yeah, I can't sit around here anymore and watch them — *(gestures to audience)* — watching us. I gotta get out of here.

ZIPPO: If you try to leave, I'll shoot you.

ZIPPO pulls gun on STALE FRY.

BLISTER-PACK: If you shoot him, I'll shoot you.

BLISTER-PACK pulls gun on ZIPPO. BUTTERSCOTCH ducks out of sight. SLURPEE points his gun at BLISTER-PACK. WET WIPE aims his gun at SLURPEE.

BLISTER-PACK: This escalated quickly.

STALE FRY: What do I do?

ZIPPO: Sit down and everything'll be cool whip.

SLURPEE: I'm gonna shoot anyway.

Guys groan.

ZIPPO: That's not the deal, Slurpee.

BLISTER-PACK: Has anyone ever been in a Mexican standoff that hasn't ended in bloodshed?

STALE FRY: This is my first standoff.

SLURPEE: And it'll be your last.

ZIPPO: *(to SLURPEE)* C'mon, man, think of Mitzi.

SLURPEE bellows and shoots BLISTER-PACK. The guys fire their guns. The guys all collapse dead.

BUTTERSCOTCH reappears from his hiding spot with his own gun drawn. Mobile phone rings.

BUTTERSCOTCH: *(on phone)* Yeah, boss? …Wait a minute, is this Mitzi? How ya doin', doll? Zippo? He's gone — they're all gone — dead. Yep. Mexican standoff again. Say… you still got that old Mustang? Would you mind swinging by to pick me up? Wet Wipe was my ride…

END OF SCENE. BLACK OUT.

BODY IN THE LIBRARY

A cast of dozens marvel over a body being found in a manor's library

<u>CAST</u>:
THE MAID
LORD BLITHERING - *dressed in pajamas and dressing gown*
LADY BLITHERING - *dressed in nightgown and dressing gown*
THE BUTLER
MILKMAN
CONSTABLE
VICAR ON A BICYCLE
AUNT AGATHA - *Lady Blithering's aunt*
OLD BIDDY
SMARMY MAN
OLD MAN WITH EAR TRUMPET
DELIVERY BOY
THE COOK
NEWSBOY
TOUR GUIDE
A Cluster of Tourists (5 people, non-Speaking)
DETECTIVE INSPECTOR
HERCULE POIROT
DR. FRANKENSTEIN
BLONDE FLAPPER

SETTING: *The foyer of a grand manor. The front door is stage left, the entry to the library is stage right, the staircase and entrances from the kitchen and elsewhere upstage of the staircase*

THE MAID *screams offstage.*
LORD BLITHERING *and* LADY BLITHERING *come rushing downstairs into the foyer as* THE MAID *scrambles out of the library.*

THE MAID: There's a body in the library!

LORD BLITHERING: A body?

LADY BLITHERING: In the library?

THE MAID: There's a body in the library.

LORD BLITHERING: In the *library*?

LADY BLITHERING: Our library? A body?

LORD BLITHERING and LADY BLITHERING lean into the library doorway to peer into the room.

LORD BLITHERING: There *is* a body in the library!

LADY BLITHERING: A body! Good heavens!

THE MAID dials the telephone and whispers soundlessly into the receiver. THE BUTLER enters.

LADY BLITHERING: The maid just said there's a body in the library.

LORD BLITHERING: And there is a body — in *my* library!

THE BUTLER: There was no body in the library earlier.

LADY BLITHERING: There is a body in the library *now*! *(gestures to the library entrance)*

THE BUTLER moves to look in the library.

THE BUTLER: Oh, that's a *body*!

THE MILKMAN enters and sets milk on table in foyer. Curious to see what all the hubbub is about, he peers through the library door.

THE MILKMAN: Say, that's *some* body in there. Hubba-hubba!

THE CONSTABLE enters.

THE CONSTABLE: Wot's all this about a body in the library?

LORD BLITHERING: The maid found a body in *our* library.

THE CONSTABLE exits through library. The VICAR rides in on a bicycle.

VICAR: There's a *body* in the library?

AUNT AGATHA enters.

AUNT AGATHA: Oh, dear niece, a body in your library — *how exciting*!

A group of townspeople wander in — OLD BIDDY, SMARMY MAN, and OLD MAN WITH AN EAR TRUMPET. The foyer is crowded as the characters linger in the room, occasionally rubbernecking around to look into the library. THE CONSTABLE is, so far, the only character in the library (offstage) with the body.

OLD BIDDY: A body *in* the library?

SMARMY MAN: *A* body in the library?

OLD MAN WITH AN EAR TRUMPET: There's a biddy in the lavatory?

OLD BIDDY: *(to OLD MAN)* No, the bobby's in the laboratory.

A DELIVERY BOY enters.

DELIVERY BOY: Somebody order a delivery?

THE COOK enters from the kitchen.

THE COOK: Is that butter for the larder?

DELIVERY BOY nods to THE COOK, who leads him back to the kitchen. NEWSBOY enters.

NEWSBOY: Extra, extra! Body found in library of Blithering Manor.

A TOUR GUIDE enters with a cluster of tourists.

TOUR GUIDE: ...and through those doors you'll find the Blithering Manor library, where some have said there is a body.

Tourists "Ooh" and gather around the library door to take photographs. THE DETECTIVE INSPECTOR enters.

LADY BLITHERING: Inspector, there's a body *in our library*!

DETECTIVE INSPECTOR: Right.

THE DETECTIVE INSPECTOR quickly glances into the library.

DETECTIVE INSPECTOR: This is clearly a library with a body in it. Poisoned. Obviously murdered by a lover. Lord Blithering, if you'll come with me —

LORD BLITHERING begins to protest as THE DETECTIVE INSPECTOR starts to put him towards the main entrance. HERCULE POIROT enters.

HERCULE POIROT: Ah, good, everyone has arrived. You are no doubt wondering about the body in the library and I can tell you the Inspector is wrong. It —

DR. FRANKENSTEIN bursts in from the library.

DR. FRANKENSTEIN: It's alive! *(maniacal laugh)*

Crowd murmurs. A BLONDE FLAPPER emerges from the library.

BLONDE FLAPPER: *(yawns broadly)* What's all the hoopla?

LADY BLITHERING and THE MAID faint. THE DETECTIVE INSPECTOR and THE CONSTABLE harrumph and leave. The crowd murmurs amongst themselves. The tourists snap photos.

BLONDE FLAPPER: *(to HERCULE POIROT)* Oh hiya, Herky! Say, is there any grub? I'm starved! That was some party last night, huh? I tells ya, when I pass out, I'm dead to the world! *(screeching, braying laugh)* Fancy digs, these. Where am I?

A gunshot comes from the library. The BLONDE FLAPPER falls forward to the floor. The rest of the crowd loudly exhales in relief.

LORD BLITHERING: *(to offstage library shooter)* Thank you!

END OF SCENE. BLACK OUT.

CAR TROUBLE

A mid-40s suburban couple encounter potential delays en route to their first official date.

<u>CAST:</u>
DIANE - early 40s middle class woman, very crisp and put together.
GREG - mid-40s middle class guy in the suburban date uniform — khakis, polo shirt and a sports coat.

SETTING: *Interior of a modest four-door sedan*

GREG is calmly driving as DIANE uses the passenger side visor mirror to reapply lipstick and check her reflection. She studies something else in the reflection, then flips the visor mirror back up.

DIANE: We're being followed.

GREG: We're not being followed.

DIANE: That car has been behind us for several miles.

GREG: Not everyone is a speed demon, Diane. Anyway, who would follow us?

DIANE peers at the outer passenger side rearview mirror.

DIANE: I don't know. *(pauses)* Oh. Well—

GREG: They wouldn't.

DIANE: They could.

GREG: You don't think they know, do you?

DIANE: Dennis was curiously inquisitive tonight.

GREG: What'd you tell him?

DIANE: Book club with Martha, as usual. He hates Martha, so I know he won't talk to her.

GREG: And if he asks you about the book later?

DIANE: I'll tell him it was some French historical women's lit.

GREG: That'll zonk him right out.

DIANE: Did you tell anyone about tonight?

GREG: Nobody asked and I didn't offer.

DIANE: Maybe she doesn't need to ask because she's having you tailed.

GREG: If Gloria wanted to track my movements, she wouldn't be so subtle. She'd be crouched in the backseat or the trunk, waiting for her gotcha moment.

DIANE turns to check the backseat. GREG puts his arm out to block her.

GREG: You'd smell her perfume — Odious Rex. A foul stench for a foul woman.

DIANE: What about work? Would one of your clients feel compelled to follow you?

GREG: I'm a vet. I didn't kill anyone's cat today, so I think we're good.

DIANE: Good.

GREG: Maybe one of your co-workers has it out for you? Maybe Martha's tired of being your alibi and wants to see what's going on.

DIANE turns to look out rear window and squints at the car behind.

DIANE: *(sighs with relief)* It's not her car.

GREG: Maybe she rented a car.

DIANE: Stop it!

GREG: You're really getting upset over this?

They drive in silence for a beat. DIANE lightly fidgets, glancing out at the rearview mirror. As GREG reaches out to soothe her, DIANE nervously flinches.

GREG: You know, just because a car is behind us doesn't mean it's following us. We've been behind this same car for almost as many miles but we're not necessarily following them.

DIANE: What are the odds that three cars in a row would be travelling the same direction for ten miles, without changing lanes or adjusting speed?

GREG: It's just coincidence. Dennis and Gloria are not having us followed because they suspect we're having an affair. The car in front of us just happens to look like Gloria's cherry red Camaro. Look next to us, it's the same SUV that's tried passing us twice and behind them is the moving van that I'm sure was right behind us a few minutes ago. This is what traffic is like, babe.

DIANE: …Hmm.

GREG: Okay?

DIANE: That's our exit coming up, right?

GREG: It is! See, we'll shake these guys and everything'll be fine.

GREG motions to change to the right exit lane.

DIANE: *(points to car ahead)* We've got company.

GREG: It's still coincidence.

DIANE: They're going to think we're following them.

GREG: They probably haven't even noticed us.

DIANE: *(looks out the back window)* We're still being followed by that car, too.

GREG: Diane—

DIANE: I know, I sound paranoid.

GREG: Maybe we'll lose 'em at this intersection.

DIANE: Oh, God! We're in the middle of a chase!

GREG: I'm not sure it's a chase if everyone's going the speed limit, darling.

A beat as they drive through the intersection.

GREG: Okay, through the intersection and the gang's still here.

DIANE: On television, the good investigators always keep at least one car between them and whoever they're tailing, so they're not so conspicuous.

GREG: Do you want to divert? If I get us out of this processional, we can finally see who's really following who.

DIANE: Now you think we're being followed.

GREG: I didn't say that. I'm gonna try to pass this guy, alright?

GREG motions to switch to left lane and struggles to accelerate to pass the Camaro.

GREG: *(becomes increasingly irritated)* Oh, c'mon! Let me go around, you fucker. What's your problem? You got your sweet little midlife muscle car — because a sensible four-door sedan was too safe and boring for you — and you have the gall to drive the speed limit when you could've been miles ahead by now. Why don't you drive off a fucking cliff?!

DIANE: *(peering into the windows of the Camaro as they try passing)* They've got some seriously tinted windows. Who does that? Dirty criminals, I bet. *(to the Camaro)* What's your racket? Drugs? Murder? What did you do to have a plainclothes detective tail you in an unmarked car?

GREG: I don't think she's gonna let me get around.

DIANE: What if we try turning off onto a side street? Is there an alley we can cut through? Or an open cargo truck we can drive up into?

GREG: Is it possible you watch too many crime dramas?

DIANE: Dennis records them all on the PVR and likes to watch them during dinner. God forbid we eat at a table and have an actual conversation like normal people.

GREG: Actually, I think eating in front of the television has become the norm for most people.

DIANE: I know it seemed old fashioned but I miss the tradition. Eating at a table just feels more civilized than balancing a plate on your lap while slumped into a couch.

GREG slams his hands on the steering wheel and roars in frustration.

DIANE: What's the matter? Something I said?

GREG: Oh, no. I'm so aggravated by this…whatever it is we're stuck in.

GREG steers sharply to make a right-hand turn down a side street.

GREG: There. We lost 'em.

DIANE: Finally!

GREG: Now, let's go have a romantic dinner just the two of us with no more complications. We'll get a bottle of wine, have a little conversation, eat lobster by the tiny tea-light candle that passes for ambience…

DIANE glances out the side rearview mirror.

DIANE: The Camaro is following us.

GREG: No.

DIANE: See for yourself.

GREG looks more closely in his rearview mirror.

GREG: What the hell?! *(shouting at the mirror to Camaro)* Go find someone else to play your game!

DIANE: We are going to be murdered.

GREG: We are not going to be murdered.

DIANE: We will have to stop eventually and these people are going to kill us and chop us into bits and Gloria will suffocate in the trunk.

GREG: We will not be killed. Gloria's not in the trunk.

DIANE: Well, do we call the police?

GREG: And tell them what? We're two people having an affair who happen to be caught in the middle of an inexplicable chase scene while en route to consummate our affair?

DIANE: Do we have to tell them that part? It sounds so sleazy.
And what if they call Dennis?

DIANE turns to look at the driver of this car.

DIANE: The headlights are too bright to see who's in that car. Wait, did you say Gloria has a car like that?

GREG: Yeah. so?

DIANE: Are you sure it's not?

GREG: I don't think it's her license plate.

DIANE: She could've gotten a new one?

GREG: Diane, do you think we were following Gloria and now she's following us?

DIANE: …Maybe.

GREG: What about the other car from before? Where'd he go?

DIANE: I, I don't know.

GREG: Oh, I know! He was the private investigator I hired to follow Gloria because she's cheating on me!

DIANE: Okay, Greg. I'm sorry. I took it too far. I'm just nervous about tonight and it's gotten the better of me. Of course, we're not being followed. We're not in trouble. I'm sorry for being so paranoid.

GREG: No. No, you were right. That is Gloria.

DIANE: Greg!

GREG: And I did pay a guy to follow her.

DIANE: Then why were we following her, too?

GREG: That actually was a coincidence.

DIANE: I can't believe this!

GREG: You could just a second ago when you thought of it.

DIANE: Are you using me to get back at her?

GREG: Are you using me to get back at Dennis?

DIANE: No — what do you mean? What?

GREG: Oh, like you don't know?!

DIANE: Know what?

GREG: Dennis and Gloria are together. Mr. "TV dinner" and Ms. "flashy roadster" have been seeing each other for six months. Are you telling me that for all the detective procedurals you watch, you were completely clueless?

DIANE: I guess I was.

GREG: Oh, god. Diane, I'm sorry. I'm sorry, okay? Ah, sh—. I messed up. We were so good! This, us? I mean, whatever they're doing is, ergh — but I liked us. I like you. I really like you, Diane. Please, tell me I didn't ruin this.

DIANE: I want to go home.

GREG: I'm so sorry.

DIANE: I am an idiot. Embarrassed. Stupid. Idiot.

GREG: Let's be idiots together.

DIANE: What an absolute cliché. I thought Dennis was the clueless boob and I felt so guilty leaving him to fall asleep in front of the television alone tonight. Poor lonely, inattentive, stupid Dennis thinks his wife is out at a book club meeting when she's really off to schtup his poker buddy! Har-dee-fucking-har.

GREG: I don't even really like to play poker.

DIANE: Not helping.

GREG looks up in rearview mirror.

GREG: Hey, look behind us.

DIANE: *(checks the rearview mirror)* We're not being followed anymore.

GREG: They gave up on us again.

DIANE *sighs.*

GREG: What about you?

DIANE: Am I giving up on us? Is there really an us?

GREG: *(reaches over and grabs her hand)* I would very much like there to be an us.

DIANE: Let's discuss it over dinner. We've still got that reservation.

GREG: Hey, I've got a few reservations myself.

DIANE: About that private investigator—

GREG: Is he following us again?!

DIANE: No. Is he single?

END OF SCENE. BLACK OUT.

THE CONSULTATION

A nebbish man in the midst of a life crisis seeks guidance from a tattoo artist to make a lasting impression.

CAST:
HAROLD - customer, a middle-aged man, clueless and nebbish
HUGH - tattoo artist, gruff but kind

SETTING: *A vintage-inspired tattoo studio*

A bell above the shop door jingles as HAROLD enters the tattoo studio.

HAROLD: Good morning.

HUGH: Good morning.

HAROLD: Are you the Hugh of Hugh's Tattoos?

HUGH: I am.

HAROLD: Excellent. I'd like to get a tattoo, please.

HUGH: Where would you like to get it?

HAROLD: Erm, in this shop, I thought.

HUGH: You've come to the right place.

HAROLD: Splendid.

HUGH: Please, have a seat.

HAROLD: Thank you.

The men take seats on opposite sides of a table.

HUGH: Have you thought about what kind of tattoo you want?

HAROLD: Oh, probably the permanent kind.

HUGH: That is one of the more common choices. Do you know what sort of design you would like?

HAROLD: Ah. I hadn't considered. Do you have a recommendation?

HUGH: I can show you the standards — the skull and crossbones, serpents and flames, a traditional tribute to dear ol' mom is always a favourite. We've got classic cartoon characters, tribal markings, signs of the devil, pin-up girls, seductive mermaids, dolphins, old-timey sailing ships, anchors — well, anything nautical is popular. For your body type, I would avoid, let's see, butterflies, foliage of any sort, and emojis. But it really is an individual decision.

HAROLD: Phew! So many choices! Do you have a tattoo-of-the-day special?

HUGH: No.

HAROLD: What about any sales? Any clearance bin tattoo designs?

HUGH: No.

HAROLD: Well, that does make it tough to narrow down the options.

HUGH: No worries. Lots of people who stop in here have no idea what they want. We've prepared a questionnaire specifically for people like you. Would you mind if I ask a few personal questions, to see if I can make a more fitting suggestion?

HAROLD: Of course.

HUGH picks up a clipboard, clicks the button of his retractable pen, and scribbles a few notes.

HUGH: Name?

HAROLD: Harold Jonesmith.

HUGH: Now, Harold… Why do you want a tattoo?

HAROLD: My girlfriend Henrietta just left me.

HUGH: Sorry about that, mate. Were you together long?

HAROLD: Just shy of 22 years.

HUGH: Wow! She finally gave you the ol' ultimatum, eh?

HAROLD: Her husband finally caught us. Anyway, I thought I'd shake things up a bit, start a brave new chapter in my life. I decided it's time to tackle items on the bucket list, you know, like join a group of bikers, get a tattoo, learn Esperanto, go running with the Bulls in Chicago, sleep with the fishes, take a brine-tasting tour, spend the night in a haunted mansion, climb Mount Vesuvius, go sponge diving off the coast of Florida—

HUGH: That's, erm, quite the list.

HAROLD: Isn't it?! Well, yesterday, I found a biker gang willing to take me on. So, now, it's onto the ink!

HUGH: You ride?

HAROLD: Oh, occasionally. Not as much as I'd like, of course. The roads aren't terribly accommodating to our lot, you know.

HUGH: What kind of bike do you have?

HAROLD: I just bought myself a real top-of-the-line model with a leather seat, chrome finish, all the premium features—cup holders, GPS, DVD player, seat warmer.

HUGH: We do offer discounts to a couple of local biker gangs. Which one have you joined?

HAROLD: The… hmm, I have their card in my pocket — ah, here we are — the North Islington Cycling Enthusiasts.

HUGH: Cycling enthusiasts?

HAROLD: Yes. An athletic-looking group of lads. They seem quite nice.

HUGH: So, you've joined a bicycle collective?

HAROLD: They call themselves bikers.

HUGH: I'm afraid they don't qualify for our motorcycle gang discount program.

HAROLD: Oh. That's all right.

HUGH: Have you considered getting a cycling-themed tattoo?

HAROLD: Do you think it would it make me look tough on my bike?

HUGH: Erm, it's not the usual aesthetic, but I'm sure you'll make it work. Are you looking to get a design that you can show off?

HAROLD: Yes. Well, I suppose I'd like something reasonably tasteful that I can display on the weekend. I do have a day job, so perhaps nothing on the face or neck.

HUGH: What do you do?

HAROLD: I'm a door-to-door efficiency expert.

HUGH: I didn't know there was much demand for that.

HAROLD: There isn't.

HUGH: I suppose knuckle tats are out. Hmm. *(makes notes on a clipboard)* Okay. Do you have any special interests or hobbies?

HAROLD: Making Henrietta happy was my sole purpose in life. Her interests were my interests, her wishes were my commands, her passions were my passion. Without her, I'm a bit of a tabula rasa.

HUGH: Well, think back to a time before Henrietta. Did you have a favourite film or novel?

HAROLD: I've never been keen on fiction.

HUGH: How about a favourite TV series?

HAROLD: I've never owned a television.

HUGH: Favourite cocktail?

HAROLD: I don't drink.

HUGH: Favourite food?

HAROLD: I don't enjoy eating.

HUGH: Favourite sport?

HAROLD: I don't follow athletics.

HUGH: Beloved family pet?

HAROLD: I'm allergic to animals.

HUGH: Favourite colour?

HAROLD: I'm colourblind.

HUGH: Religious?

HAROLD: Not particularly.

HUGH: Any political affiliation?

HAROLD: I'd rather not say.

HUGH: Do you have a favourite word?

HAROLD: No.

HUGH: Favourite shape?

HAROLD: Mnh-mm.

HUGH: Lucky number?

HAROLD: Zero.

HUGH: Esteemed idol?

HAROLD: Nada.

HUGH: Prized possession?

HAROLD: Afraid not.

HUGH: Preferred brand of soap?

HAROLD: Zilch.

HUGH: Cherished childhood memory?

HAROLD: Nope.

HUGH: Favourite board game? Typeface? Insect? Time of day? Historical era? Building material? Favourite President of the United States?!

HAROLD: No. Sorry.

HUGH slams down his clipboard and pen. He takes a deep breath to keep his temper in check.

HUGH: Did you love your mother?

HAROLD: I'm an orphan.

HUGH: Phew! You weren't kidding about being a blank slate!

HAROLD: I'm sorry. I'm not being much of a help, am I? Not very efficient of us, Harold. Tsk.

HUGH: There must be something from your life we can use. How about — what's your astrological sign?

HAROLD: I was never taken in by astrology. Following horoscopes isn't exactly an economical use of time. Let's say the average person takes thirty seconds a day to review the newspaper horoscope, perhaps longer for a weekly forecast. They're losing fifteen to twenty minutes a month that could have been applied to actual self-betterment, like learning a new language or balancing their bankbook. Pfft! Anyway, horoscopes are hardly ever accurate.

HUGH: A Capricorn would say that.

HAROLD: *(gasps)* How'd you guess?!

HUGH: Astrological tattoos are our biggest seller. One learns to read the signs.

HAROLD: I see. Well, ah, for curiosity's sake, what is the symbol for Capricorn?

HUGH: A sea-goat.

HAROLD: Sea goat?

HUGH: Yes. It's a half-goat, half-fish mythological hybrid creature.

HAROLD: Like a mer-goat?

HUGH: Exactly. It's based in part on the Sumerian god of wisdom. You're a bit of a wise guy yourself. What do you think?

HAROLD: Enh, I can't quite picture myself biking through brine country whilst sporting a mer-goat on my ankle.

HUGH: I can't picture that myself, mate.

HAROLD: Oh, I don't know! Maybe I'm not the tattoo type. What if I choose something and hate it? I'll be permanently disfigured! Will this lead down a slippery slope of bad decisions? What will I do next—get nipple piercings and a perm? Join a cult? Become a professional ghost hunter? Buy a condo? Where does it end? All of a sudden, I'll be an angry biker with a fro-hawk living in an urban commune surrounded by spirits from the netherworld because I got a tattoo of a guppy with goat legs!

A dejected HAROLD sighs and repeatedly thumps his forehead against the table.

HUGH: Look, we've got some temporary tattoos here that we give to children. Why don't you take a few, try them out on various parts of your body, get some ideas in your head. If you find you're still keen on getting inked up, come back round and we'll sketch up some designs for you.

HAROLD: I appreciate your effort, Hugh, but let's face it, I need this tattoo like a fish needs a bicycle. It was very silly for me to come in here and waste your time. Good day.

HUGH: That's it!

HAROLD: *(resigned)* That's it.

HUGH: No. A fish riding a bike — that's you. That's your tattoo!

HAROLD: Yes? Of course! Wait! No! Abraham Lincoln!

HUGH: A fish riding Abraham Lincoln?

HAROLD: No, no. Abraham Lincoln riding a bicycle — a penny-farthing!

HUGH: Abraham Lincoln riding a penny-farthing. Right. Good.

HAROLD: Ah—! Abraham Lincoln with a mermaid tail riding a penny-farthing. He'll be my guiding force up Mount Vesuvius.

HUGH: You'll be the toast of Pompeii!

HAROLD: Wait'll the chaps of the North Islington Cycling Enthusiasts get a load of me.

HUGH: Are you ready?

HAROLD: Yes!

HUGH: Let's get started.

HUGH fires up a tattoo gun while HAROLD unzips his trousers.

END OF SCENE. BLACK OUT.

DEEP CUTS

A couple attempts to disconnect and reconnect on a weekend getaway.

<u>CAST</u>:
SOPHIE - *(early 30s), young Millennial*
SAM - *(mid 30s), old Millennial*

SETTING: *An Airbnb guest house, sparsely decorated with old analog technology.* SOURCE MUSIC: *Electric Light Orchestra, Out of the Blue (songs: "Standin' in the Rain", "Big Wheels", "Summer and Lightning", "Mr. Blue Sky")*

SAM crouches in front of a vintage turntable, fumbling with the knobs and setting the needle onto the record. SOPHIE watches from her spot on the sofa.

SOPHIE: Sam, do you know what you're doing?

SAM: No, but I saw somebody use one of these on TV. How hard can it be?

SOPHIE: I didn't even know a suitcase could play music.

SAM: It's not a suitcase, it's a portable record player.

SOPHIE: *(rolls her eyes)* I was joking?

The music starts.

SAM: Voila!

SAM joins SOPHIE on the couch.

SOPHIE: Now what?

SAM: We listen.

SOPHIE: Okay.

They sit and listen to the music for a beat. SOPHIE picks up her phone. SAM winces and groans.

SOPHIE: No?

SAM: Well, we're on a getaway. The purpose of the trip is to Get Away. If we're on our phones, are we really getting away from anything?

SOPHIE: *(puts her phone down)* Fine. We'll do a digital detox.

SAM: Right? We'll take a little break from our screens; just enjoy the music and each other's company.

SOPHIE: What are we listening to?

SAM retrieves album cover and reads it.

SAM: Electric Light Orchestra, *Out of the Blue*. Never heard of it.

SOPHIE: Is this rock opera?

SAM: I don't know. There's a spaceship on the cover. It looked better than the other choices.

SOPHIE sifts through the other record albums on the table.

SOPHIE: *Mountain Music Jamboree, Colonel Sanders' Tijuana Picnic, American Gospel Disco* — is this meant to be ironic? Are hipsters still doing irony?

SAM: I hadn't considered this to be a hipster kind of place. Maybe the owners just have weird taste in music.

SOPHIE: *(gesturing to unseen props and decor)* They are for sure trying hard for that hipster vibe — the Edison light bulbs, the old typewriter they're using as a guest book — they spent a lot of money on Etsy to look like they just raided a salvage yard.

SAM: It is very Instagram-friendly. But it's got some character at least. You're probably not going to find a shelf of antique cameras in a Travelodge.

They sit in silence while the record plays.

SOPHIE: Did people really ever just sit and listen to music?

SAM: Of course! I mean, probably. I've seen pictures.

SOPHIE: I get inviting friends over for a dance party. People just sitting around the record player seems kinda lame. What's the point of music if you can't bop to it?

SAM: What are you — are you picturing a bunch of old Victorian academics in leather wingback chairs, silently puffing on pipes while the gramophone plays?

SOPHIE chuckles. SAM starts bobbing his head to the music.

SAM: Even stuffy academics must've tapped their toes to the beat once in a while.

SOPHIE: Not to this record.

SOPHIE reaches for her phone. SAM clears his throat.

SAM: You just said we're on a digital detox here.

SOPHIE: I know. I wanted to look up this Electronic Orchestra Company on Wikipedia.

SAM: You'll have to make do with reading the album cover. No social media, no texting, no gaming. Besides, there's no wi-fi here.

SOPHIE: What did people do before the Internet?

SAM: Played board games. Made love. Did drugs. Talked.

SOPHIE: Did you bring Monopoly? LSD?

SAM: Nope, sorry. There's probably some vintage cocaine hidden in one of those film canisters.

SOPHIE: *(getting restless)* Bleh. Ugh! Can we at least skip this song? It's so boring. No... pretentious. Pretentious and boring.

SAM: We committed to listening to this record from start to finish, for better or worse.

SOPHIE: Did we?

SAM: If we skip this song, who's to say you won't want to skip the next one, or the one after? And then, what's the point? Let's just see how it plays out. Maybe, by the end, we'll have discovered our new favourite band!

SOPHIE: Unlikely.

SAM: We're really spoiled, you know. We have virtually unlimited access to everything under the sun, literally at our fingertips. We could have all sorts of new experiences, but we're stuck... scrolling through the same old apps, listening to the same songs we loved when we were kids. There's so much to explore but here we are, swiping left on everything that doesn't instantly wow us.

SOPHIE: Okay, settle down, grandpa. You've been reading too many Millennial-bashing Boomer takes online again.

SAM: But, are they right though? Am I too caught up in my own bubble to give new things — or old things — a chance? What amazing stuff am I missing out on because it's easier to fall back on old familiar favourites?

SOPHIE: A new girlfriend, maybe.

SAM: When was the last time you listened to an album all the way through?

SOPHIE: I don't know —

SAM: Well, now's our chance, to experience a band we don't know, to hear their music the way they intended it to be heard. These songs are probably in a certain order for a reason, and we should try to respect that.

SOPHIE: You don't know how to skip songs on a record, do you?

SAM: …Be gentle, I'm a vinyl virgin.

SOPHIE: Okay, I'll change it. Don't you just lift the needle or something?

SOPHIE starts to get up, SAM stops her.

SAM: No!

SOPHIE: What?!

SAM: I'm sorry you hate it, but I'm actually enjoying it. When we're back home, I may get a copy for myself.

SOPHIE: Fine.

SAM: You'd rather listen to *Colonel Sanders' Tijuana Picnic*?

SOPHIE: God, I can't even! I'd rather sit in silence!

SAM: Okay, I give up — what is your problem with this record?

SOPHIE: This record? It's just too... perfect?

SAM: It's too good?

SOPHIE: It's too much, like, too polished and slick. It sounds like... classical music for robots. Like this guest house... every bit is strategically placed. Everything looks like it was done on purpose but... like, why?

SAM: I dunno. I like it.

SOPHIE: I'm just saying, it's all very nice and tidy but it doesn't feel authentic.

SAM: I didn't know authenticity was important to you.

SOPHIE: There's a lot you don't know about me.

SAM: Even after three years and that extremely detailed dating profile?

SOPHIE: Some things are too complex for eCupid.

SAM: Well, that's why we're here, now. For us to reconnect, get to know each other better. Now that I think about it, I really don't know anything about your childhood... or your favourite song. What was the first album you ever owned?

SOPHIE: *(getting uncomfortable)* Can't we watch a movie instead? There must be a steam-powered DVD player somewhere around here.

SAM: You don't want to talk to me?

SOPHIE: While the record is still playing?

SAM: Yeah, we don't have to sit here in silence. You don't like it, we'll let it play in the background.

SOPHIE: Enh.

SAM: Come on, Sophie, I'm really trying here.

SOPHIE: You're trying my patience.

SAM gets up and storms off to the other side of the room.

SAM: Okay. You want a movie? Here, I've got a movie for you — Picture a nice couple cuddling beneath the warm glow of the Edison bulbs in a romantic midcentury bungalow. They're listening to a record album… it's a band they've never heard of and the music's kinda weird but they're enjoying the experience. The boyfriend says, "darling, It feels like we've known each other forever and yet, there's still so much I don't know about you. Tell me, what was the first record you ever owned?" The girlfriend gets a little shy and giggles, "Promise you won't laugh?" He says, "I swear — I won't! Was it a boy band?" She gets huffy, "I'll have you know that some boy bands are very talented!" He confesses that his first record was a boy band, The Monkees Greatest Hits, which his mom got for his tenth birthday. "No! What a coincidence!" The girlfriend exclaims, "I, too, had The Monkees Greatest Hits, on cassette and wore it out from playing it so much." They both chuckle and agree that The Monkees were the best boy band of all, but argue over who was dreamiest — for the record, she says Micky and he goes, surprisingly, with Peter. Our couple reminisce into the night about all the movie soundtracks and greatest hits albums they both listened to, each realizing that they've never actually listened to an original album by any band, being so used to singles and compilations.

The couple are delighted by this newfound bond, pleased to be sharing secrets and new experiences. It's a story they'll go on to tell their children — well, it's something they'll brag about smugly at next week's brunch with their other couple friends.

SOPHIE earnestly applauds SAM's performance.

SAM: I'll tell you what doesn't happen. The girlfriend doesn't pout about everything and admit that she'd rather stare at a screen instead of spending one intimate moment with her pretentious, boring boyfriend!

SAM picks up a record album and moves to throw it. SOPHIE jumps up and stops him.

SOPHIE: Whoa! Wait— I'm sorry. Okay? I'm really not trying to be difficult.

SAM: …Okay.

SOPHIE: Can I use my phone?

SAM: *(shrugs defeatedly)* Why not!

SOPHIE: I know, it'll just take a second. Look.

SOPHIE picks up her phone and SAM watches disbelievingly as she taps and swipes. SOPHIE passes her phone to SAM.

SOPHIE: That's my playlist.

SAM: *(scrolls through the list on SOPHIE's phone)* It's all podcasts. So what?

SOPHIE: You don't think it's weird that I have no music on my phone?

SAM: Like, no music? *(swipes and scrolls on the phone)* Wow, there's literally not one song on here.

SOPHIE: I don't… enjoy music. I mean, I can't.

SAM: Oh. Okay… is it a medical condition or—?

SOPHIE: My father was a radio DJ for a popular FM rock station in my hometown. He had ambitions — and a lot of groupies. When I was four years old, he was promoted to a prime time slot and he abandoned me and my mom and brothers because it was "better for his public image" to be single. We couldn't leave town, so we were stuck hearing his voice everywhere. We couldn't listen to the radio to keep up with the Top 40 hits. Eventually it was too painful to listen to music at all because it reminded us of him. So, we started listening to AM talk radio at home and I never developed an interest in music. Now my playlist is all TED talks and comedy podcasts.

SAM: God! How awful!

SOPHIE: Like, I know I can't avoid all music, it's literally everywhere. I've lost friends because they wanna get loose at the clubs and I'm out here blasting Judge John Hodgman in my headphones at the grocery store so I don't start sobbing in the soup aisle when "MMMBop" plays on the satellite radio. This is so embarrassing! It sounds stupid when I say it out loud now. I'm a grown-up. I should be able to listen to a pop song without getting uncomfortable. I should be able to listen to whatever this is.

SAM: Aww, honey! It's not stupid. *(moves to hug SOPHIE)* I think I saw a Shelley Berman record in the pile?

SOPHIE: Maybe later.

SAM: Look, you never have to hear this damned thing again!

SAM picks up the ELO album cover and starts to tear it in half but feels the second LP in the sleeve.

SOPHIE: You don't have to do that, Sam.

SAM: Why is this— Oh. Damn.

SOPHIE: What's wrong?

SAM pulls out other record and examines the label. He erupts into laughter.

SOPHIE: What? What's the big joke?

SAM: *(still laughing)* This is a double album. It has two records.

SOPHIE: Oh. And so…?

SAM: I put on the second album. We started in the middle. So much for "we're gonna listen to this whole thing whether we like it or not".

SOPHIE: You wouldn't want to start over?

SAM: No, we're done.

SAM goes to turn off the record player. ELO's "Mr. Blue Sky" starts. SOPHIE perks up.

SOPHIE: Ooh — wait. Do I know this? *(starts bobbing head and bouncing)* Oh…it bops! I like it. Leave it on!

SAM: Really? You wanna—

SOPHIE: You were about to destroy these records for me. I owe it to you to give it a chance.

SAM: You don't have to—

SOPHIE: Like you said, let's see how it plays out. Maybe this can be our song. Dance party?

SAM: Dance party.

SAM and SOPHIE join hands and start to dance.

END OF SCENE. BLACK OUT.

EINE KLEINE FAHRSTUHLMUSIK

The eternal struggle to bring art and entertainment to the general public has a building manager at odds with a piano player and his emotional support raccoon.

<u>CAST</u>:
OLIVIA - *the building manager*
CLIVE - *the pianist*

Liberace — *a raccoon (unseen)*

SETTING: *The elevator bay in the lobby of a high-rise bank building*

OLIVIA stands next to bank of elevator doors. She presses call button. Doors open to reveal CLIVE seated at a baby grand piano inside the elevator. CLIVE is improvising on the piano.

OLIVIA: Excuse me.

CLIVE: Hi there. Any requests?

OLIVIA: This is inappropriate.

CLIVE: I don't know that one; is it Gershwin?

OLIVIA: Where are you going?

CLIVE: Nowhere to go but up.

OLIVIA: What do you think you're doing?

CLIVE: What does it look like?

OLIVIA: It looks like you're playing a piano in an elevator.

CLIVE: Mystery solved!

OLIVIA: What business do you have in this building?

CLIVE: This is my business.

CLIVE plays the opening bars of "There's No Business Like Show Business". OLIVIA interrupts.

OLIVIA: Piano playing in the bank elevator is not a job.

CLIVE: I'm a troubadour. I bring my music to people I feel need it most.

OLIVIA: A noble cause — but, a piano? It's too big, wider than the doors even. How'd you get it in here?

CLIVE: A little imagination can get you anywhere.

CLIVE plays the opening bars to "Pure Imagination" from the Willy Wonka & the Chocolate Factory *soundtrack. OLIVIA interrupts.*

OLIVIA: Look, if we want music in this lift, we'll put in a radio.

CLIVE: Not the same as live music.

OLIVIA: True, but your piano is limiting the quantity of people that can be carried between floors.

CLIVE: It is boosting the *quality* of people.

OLIVIA: There's also the weight to consider. Elevators have weight limits and I'm sure you're exceeding it.

CLIVE: My piano weighs 500 pounds. If a person weighed that much, would you prevent them from riding this elevator?

OLIVIA: Possibly.

CLIVE: That's discrimination.

OLIVIA: Have you considered the fact that you're impeding on the rights of the mobility-challenged?

CLIVE: Nah — plenty of canes and wheelchairs have passed through here. In fact, they were my best tippers.

CLIVE plays generic cocktail music.

OLIVIA: Sir, this is a passenger elevator, not a cocktail lounge.

CLIVE: People seem to be enjoying the music. Let the music-haters take the other lift.

OLIVIA: We're not asking people to do that.

CLIVE: Why not? You have smoking and non-smoking elevators don't you?

OLIVIA: All elevators are non-smoking. *(sniffs)* You haven't been smoking in here?!

CLIVE: Boy, you're just laying down all kinds of rules — no music, no smoking, no smuggling a dead body in the piano, no setting off fireworks in the elevator shaft. Next, you'll be saying —

OLIVIA: Do I need to call the police?

CLIVE: — something like that.

OLIVIA: Did you say there's a dead body in your piano?

CLIVE: No.

OLIVIA: You intimated.

CLIVE: I hypothesized.

OLIVIA: Look, you're turning this place inside out — breaking all kinds of building ordinances and by-laws as it is. If you're transporting human remains—

CLIVE stops playing.

CLIVE: Whoa! I never said human.

OLIVIA: If I look inside your piano, am I going to find a dead body?

CLIVE: Probably not. I mean, you might find Liberace, my emotional support raccoon. He curled up in there to take a nap a few hours ago and, well, he hasn't popped out since. I've been too scared to check on him, to tell you the truth.

OLIVIA cautiously raises the piano lid, recoiling in anticipation of finding something awful.

OLIVIA: *(sighs with relief)* He's fine. *(watches the raccoon)* Aww, he's so cute — look at him eating pretzels off his chubby wittle belly!

CLIVE: Oh, thank goodness! Wait — I was saving those for lunch, Libby!

OLIVIA continues watching the raccoon with delight for a beat longer, then snaps back to business.

OLIVIA: Enough! You and your raccoon have to leave.

CLIVE: Where do you expect me to go?

OLIVIA: A courtyard, a bus depot, the bowling alley — anywhere that isn't here.

CLIVE: Oh! No concern for your fellow man! Good job tossing a needy musician out into the street with no prospects. Brava!

CLIVE starts to play a blues riff. OLIVIA interrupts.

OLIVIA: It isn't commentary on your abilities as a musician. I love music. I took piano lessons as a kid. This just isn't the proper venue for it.

CLIVE: There's a klezmer band playing in the men's toilet on the seventh floor!

OLIVIA: They have a permit.

CLIVE: I want a permit.

OLIVIA: You cannot have a permit to play the grand piano in an elevator.

CLIVE: It's a baby grand.

OLIVIA: Oh, why didn't you say so — no.

CLIVE: How about a gig in the main lobby?

OLIVIA: I don't think so.

CLIVE: Why not?

OLIVIA: You have a wild animal living in your piano.

CLIVE: He plays a mean tambourine. The crowds love it.

OLIVIA: No.

CLIVE: What if he's wearing his costume? In his sequin jumpsuit, you can hardly tell he's a raccoon.

OLIVIA: A costume? *(eagerly)* Do you have pictures? *(regains composure)* No. Nope. It's a health and safety issue. Liberace cannot come out.

CLIVE: Again, with the discrimination. I might press charges. *(to raccoon in piano)* Libby — get my lawyer on the phone!

OLIVIA: No-no-no — You do want a permit?

CLIVE: …Yes. *(to raccoon in piano)* Sorry, Libby. This is a solo act now — stop eating my pretzels!

OLIVIA: *(sighs)* I'll see what I can do.

CLIVE: That's all I'm asking.

OLIVIA: Good. Now, will you please leave?

CLIVE: I will, soon, but — I did promise to play a little something for Carol's birthday, up on the 16th floor.

OLIVIA: Oh, gosh! It's Carol's birthday?! I totally forgot!

CLIVE: You know her?

OLIVIA: She's my fiancée.

CLIVE: Oof! Alright, get in. We'll work up an explosive number for her on the way.

OLIVIA: Fantastic! What're you waiting for — Pound those horse teeth, brother! *(steps into elevator and looks up)* What is — Fireworks in the elevator shaft?!

END OF SCENE. BLACK OUT.

EVERYTHING MUST GO

Two mannequins plot their escape from a closing department store.

<u>CAST</u>:
JUDY - female mannikin
RUDY - male mannikin
Joe - an actual dummy, does not move or talk
ANDY - security guard, human

SETTING: barren department store with minimal displays left, including a column with full-length mirrors, and several "store closing forever" and "liquidation sale" banners tacked up.

JUDY and RUDY are frozen in the middle of a ballroom dance pose with fake broad smiles plastered on their faces. lights dim and an alarm buzzes in RUDY's pocket. the two relax and pull away from each other.

RUDY: It's time.

JUDY: Everything's in place.

RUDY retrieves two large travel bags tucked around the set. JUDY sits down to remove her shoes. RUDY drops JUDY's bag near her feet, then stops to stretch his back.

RUDY: That's one part of the job I won't miss, all those long hours of posing. I am bone tired!

JUDY: We don't have bones.

RUDY: True, true!

JUDY and RUDY sort through their respective bags, pull out janitor uniforms, and change into them.

RUDY: Still, can't wait to have a bed of my own. How about you?

JUDY: I just can't wait to get out of here.

RUDY: You sure we can leave without being noticed?

JUDY: As long as we move fast.

RUDY: Should we be worried about the security cameras?

JUDY: I made a few adjustments to the monitors when I visited Andy last night.

RUDY: Ooh, Andy the security guard! Did you break the news to him?

JUDY: We… ended things.

RUDY: Did you tell him— ?

JUDY: I told him the truth — that I'm leaving my job and moving away.

RUDY: And that was enough? He didn't ask for details?

JUDY: I don't want to talk about it.

RUDY: You've been involved with him for months and, what? Does he know anything?

JUDY: I do not want to talk about it, Rudy.

RUDY: But—

JUDY: It's over now. Let's just hope he's too distracted to notice I've knocked out the video feed.

RUDY: Really broke his heart, huh?

JUDY: Stop.

RUDY: You didn't... kill him?

JUDY: No! It's just done. It's over. It's fine.

RUDY: Gee, I thought you really liked him. Maybe you're empty inside.

JUDY: We both are. Is our Lyft here yet?

RUDY: No. We might have to wait for the real janitors to leave so we can sneak out with them.

JUDY looks around anxiously.

JUDY: I didn't realize how empty the store is now. Eerie.

RUDY: Yep, end of an era. Damn millennials, killing everything.

JUDY: More like greedy capitalists killing everything for a quick profit.

RUDY: That's just business for ya. I'm sure gonna miss this place, though!

JUDY: You've been here too long.

RUDY: One of the first here, in fact — 1961 and fresh off the assembly line! We were really built to last back in those days!

JUDY: Are you getting all nostalgic again?

RUDY: Boy, think of all the times we've had here! Remember Chas and Elaine, oh! and Claudia? We had some wild times with those guys. Whatever happened to them?

JUDY: Management got rid of 'em to make room for those headless granite looking mannikins. Probably dumped in a landfill to be mauled by scavengers and seagulls.

RUDY: What's with the rude 'tude, Jude?

JUDY: I've had enough! I'm ready to finally live on my own terms. No more being ogled at all hours, no more small children camping out under my skirts to escape their parents, no more holding awkward poses when the curse wears off and the store is still open. This place was so cruel to us. Honestly, I don't know how we lasted this long.

RUDY: Life was pretty easy here, all things considered. Sure, the job had its flaws — what job doesn't? At least we didn't work in the warehouse with all that heavy lifting. We always had full run of the place after hours — take a nap in Bedding, go roller skating through Sporting Goods, watch Johnny Carson on the wall of TVs in Electronics. Except for the curse, we could live just as well as any human.

JUDY: You weren't sexually assaulted on a regular basis by staff and customers. If I had a dollar for every human who grabbed my tits, simulated sex with my inanimate body, or checked to see if I was anatomically correct, I could've bought this whole chain of stores several times over.

RUDY: Well, now, I've had more than a few wandering hands over the years. My dresser Mildred never let a day go by without saying— *(puts on smoky lady's voice)* "Yep, you're a fine piece of fibreglass, Mistah Rudy" while cupping my buttocks. *(sighs)* Boy, nothing's been the same since she retired!

JUDY: Soon we'll be retired.

RUDY: What luck you had finding that commune on the Internet, huh? Who knew there were so many enchanted mannikins still around? I can't wait to meet 'em all!

JUDY: Yes. The Internet is truly amazing.

RUDY: How can something so useful also be so evil? It's the reason we're losing our jobs and home, you know. Thanks to computers, nobody goes out shopping anymore. I remember when coming to the department store was a big deal. Humans would come in dressed in their finest and spend the whole day here. Now they come around in their pyjamas and get their underpants and bath mats delivered by robots.

JUDY: OK, grandpa.

RUDY: I'm just saying, people made an effort at one time.

JUDY: Humans are dumb. They're ridiculous!

RUDY: All humans or one in particular?

JUDY: They go around making up rules and breaking them — what's "in" and what's "out", what defines a "person", who can love whom — Some day they'll decide to bring back dress codes, department stores, passenger rail travel and we'll be right back in here modelling woollen suits and taffeta dresses.

RUDY: I do look resplendent in pink taffeta.

JUDY: How is it they get to go around deciding who's who and what's what, all the while we're forced to hide our very existence?

RUDY: They were here first?

JUDY: Fickle blood-pumpers! We're completely disposable to them. Look how they destroyed the rest of our friends without considering whether they might be alive. Here we are, about to embark on the biggest adventure of our lives and we can't fully enjoy it. Instead of flying on a plane like normal people, we have to get shoved into packing crates and shipped like cargo.

RUDY: We're at a disadvantage. We're only guaranteed sundown to sunrise. However, if we had a human companion…

JUDY: What are you getting at?

RUDY: I've heard people describe us as lifelike. Maybe if you told Andy that you've had lots of plastic surgery—

JUDY: Why do you keep bringing him up? Sometimes relationships run their course. Andy and I were just casual, a fling, a distraction. I was only using him to tamper with the security cameras anyhow. Yes, I may have developed feelings along the way. Yes, I will miss his squishy belly and his crooked smile and the way he snorts while laughing at bad jokes. I'll get over it. I have to get over it. Anyway, we'll be together, right?

RUDY: We — me and you, we?

JUDY: Of course.

RUDY: Nooooo.

JUDY: Oh. I guess I thought we were meant to be — what with our finding each other in this store, now we're running away together.

RUDY: No offense, dollface, but why would I tie myself down with you when I'm a good-looking eligible bachelor and my dating pool is about to vastly expand?

JUDY: When you put it that way—

RUDY: And there'll be plenty of fellas for you, too!

JUDY: Right, right.

RUDY: I'm sorry if you thought this was romantic.

JUDY: No, I didn't, really. I don't have those feelings for you, either. I just assumed I'd learn to love you over time.

RUDY: Well, you don't have to.

JUDY: Whew!

RUDY: We'll still be pals, though. Boy, it's exciting to think we're mere hours away from being in a community surrounded by our own kinfolk! It's a shame we have to leave poor Joe behind, though.

JUDY: I thought you hated Joe. You know, because he's not like us.

RUDY: Wha— never! Who could hate old Joe? Although, he does stand around with that blank expression all day. Look at him — what's he thinkin'? I know people think we're just modelling clothes, but really we're selling an image, a lifestyle. We've got real character, you and me. What's Joe got? In some ways I think he's the one who's really cursed.

A thud comes from off-stage. RUDY and JUDY freeze.

RUDY: *(through gritted teeth)* I'm not ready to die!

JUDY unfreezes.

JUDY: What're we doing?

RUDY unfreezes.

RUDY: Think it's time to go?

ANDY: *(off-stage)* Judy, don't go!

JUDY: Oh, drat.

ANDY rushes in.

ANDY: I know everything. I know all about you, Judy, and I don't care! I just want us to be together.

JUDY: How do you know?

ANDY: Well, I mean, I've worked here for a long time. There are no secrets for security guards.

RUDY: Ooh, we're all gonna have some explaining to do. Hi, I'm Rudy. Have we met?

ANDY: Andy. I think I saw you trying to hide inside a refrigerator when I was on patrol.

RUDY: I would've fit if it weren't for those darn roller skates.

ANDY and RUDY shake hands.

ANDY: Firm grip! Wasn't expecting that. Nice.

RUDY: Thanks! Been working out. I've heard all good things about you. This one over here gushes constantly.

JUDY: I don't! Shut up, Rudy!

ANDY goes to JUDY and grabs her hands.

ANDY: You left last night before I could say anything. Look, I know we're very different, but I love you. I love that you tried to pretend that you were a busy career-woman who could only get away from work during my shifts, so we had to have all our dates here. I love how you wait until three minutes before sunrise to leave me, and then make up some bonkers excuse for going. You're brilliant, you're beautiful. You may be plastic but you've got a heart of gold.

RUDY: Awww!

JUDY: I can't stay. The store is closing forever and I won't have anywhere else to go.

ANDY: Hey, I'm out a job soon, too, and I've got nothing keeping me here. Let me go with you.

JUDY: You'd really want to live around a bunch of mannikins?

ANDY: Why not? I've worked around you guys for years.

JUDY: Oh, Andy, this is so sudden, We're just about to leave! We have all these plans!

RUDY: We can make new plans.

ANDY: Yes! See? Don't you think what we had was real?

JUDY: I don't know what's real…

RUDY's phone buzzes.

RUDY: Our ride's here.

JUDY: Crap!

RUDY: Listen, dollface, you said you wanted to travel in style and a human can help you do that. What could be better than your own personal bodyguard? Why don't you stick around and work out those details? I'll go ahead and get the lay of the land and whatnot.

RUDY's phone buzzes again.

JUDY: Oh… I can't believe I'm doing this — All right!

ANDY: Hot damn!

ANDY scoops JUDY into a passionate embrace.

RUDY: Okay, you kooky couple, I'm outta here.

JUDY pulls away from ANDY and goes to hug RUDY.

JUDY: We'll see you in a couple days.

ANDY: Bye, Rudy!

RUDY smooches JUDY on her forehead and gently nudges her back to ANDY.

RUDY: See you on the other side, Jude.

RUDY picks up his travel bag and exits. JUDY grabs ANDY's hand.

JUDY: Well, now what?

ANDY: How about we get out of here?

JUDY: I thought you'd never ask.

JUDY and ANDY hold hands and exit slowly.

ANDY: So… a whole community for enchanted mannikins? What's the story there?

JUDY: Well, it all started 200 years ago on Hudson Bay with Prince Rupert's pet narwhal, the aurora borealis, and a vengeful wizard…

END OF SCENE. BLACK OUT.

FRANKENSTEIN'S FRIAR

Frankenstein's creature performs a stand-up routine.

CAST:
FM - an awkward, possibly grotesque man with discoloured skin, dressed in modern stand-up comedian wardrobe

SETTING: *The stage of a comedy club*

FM enters and approaches the stand-up microphone with a stiff gait, shielding his eyes from the bright stage lights. He picks up the microphone, growls a few times, and clears his throat.

FM: Hiya, folks. How's everybody doing out there? Are you ready to have a good time? All right! We've got a great show for you tonight, we've scared up some really terrific entertainment. Before we get started, lemme tell ya — I went to my doctor today and told him, "Doc, I haven't been feeling myself lately." He said, "Well, who have you been feeling?" I said, "Doctor, I've got a ringing in my ears" He said, "Don't answer!" I said, "I think I broke my arm in three places." He said, "Stop going to those places." Finally, the doctor says "We need to perform surgery on your hand." I say, "Will I be able to play the piano after?" He says, "I don't see why not." And I say, "Well, I couldn't play before." *(reacts to audience groans by groaning himself)* Ugh, I'm a monster, I know. I was so ugly when I was born, Doctor Frankenstein slapped himself. I asked "Doc, why can't I have the skin of a 20 year old." He said "I was afraid you'd stretch it out." I know what you're thinking, I look like a cross between Richard Nixon and the Elephant Man. You know what? I am! *(pointing to different parts of his body)* A priest, a monk, and a rabbi were in a boat… So, I'm walking down the street, this fella comes up to me and says "You've got the same nose as a guy I knew in the Navy." I said, "Maybe I do. When did he die?" I've been told I've got the heart of an investment banker, the lungs of a coal miner, the liver of an Irish bartender. It's a miracle I'm still walking around. I told my doctor I was lonely, asked what I should do to attracts girls. He suggested I join a rock band, but I don't have an ear for music. The doctor says I've got a face only a mother could love, but I haven't got a mother. I met one girl who really carried a torch for me. The trouble is, so did the giant mob behind her. I couldn't believe my luck when a girl invited me over for a romantic candlelight dinner. We had a good time for a while but it wound up being murder for her. The doctor finally took pity on me, built for me a beautiful bride… and then he built her mother. My bride has it all — the legs of a supermodel, the face of an angel, the brains of a neurosurgeon, and the shoulders of an NFL linebacker. My bride dresses to kill. Unfortunately, she cooks the same way. What's more exasperating than a bride who can cook and won't, is a bride who can't cook and will. Not many couples can say they were made for each other and mean it. Sadly, the only thing my bride and I have in common is that we were married on the same day. I knew she was Miss Right, I just didn't know her name was Always. My bride has a split personality, and I hate both of them. My bride was afraid of the dark — until she saw me naked; now she's afraid of the light. I wouldn't say my bride is cold, but every time she opens her mouth, a little light comes on inside. I told my bride I was seeing a psychiatrist; then she told me that she's seeing a psychiatrist, two plumbers, and a bartender. My bride's not too smart; I told her our kids were spoiled… she said, "All kids smell that way." You've been a great audience! Up next, we've got a guy who's a real scream.

END OF SCENE. BLACK OUT.

GRANDPA GIRLFRIEND

A couple discusses a development that could impact their relationship.

CAST:
GIRLFRIEND - early 30s, white woman, wears bulky cardigan with pockets and big glasses on chain around neck, has mannerisms that would befit an elderly man
BOYFRIEND - early 30s, youthful casual dress, contrast from GIRLFRIEND's attire

SETTING: *A café table.*

BOYFRIEND *enters and joins his GIRLFRIEND at the table.*

BOYFRIEND: Sorry I'm late, I just got your text. What's wrong?

GIRLFRIEND: Oh, nothing's wrong.

BOYFRIEND: But you have something important to tell me?

GIRLFRIEND: *(pauses, unsure how to break the news, then announces excitedly)* I'm a Grandpa!

BOYFRIEND: Hey!— Bu— what?

GIRLFRIEND: I'm a Grandpa.

BOYFRIEND: I don't know what that means. Do you have some family that I don't know about?

GIRLFRIEND: No.

BOYFRIEND: Well, uh, did you adopt someone who has kids?

GIRLFRIEND: Of course not.

BOYFRIEND: I guess I don't understand.

GIRLFRIEND: As you know, I recently had a big birthday and that got me asking myself a lot of questions. Who am I? What am I doing with my life? What do I see for my future? I've done a lot of soul searching, trying to determine my place in the world, in society, and I've finally found it.

BOYFRIEND: *(still trying to process the concept)* A grandfather?

GIRLFRIEND: Grandpa.

BOYFRIEND: So... you want to be a grandfather? How's that gonna work? How will that affect us? Are you transitioning? Oh god! I don't know what to say without sounding insensitive. What can I say? Am I allowed to ask questions? Now I have so many questions!

GIRLFRIEND: Calm down. Obviously I'm not a literal grandfather. I'm simply self-identifying as a Grandpa because that's the lifestyle that most comfortably defines me.

BOYFRIEND: Why not be a grandmother? You could take up knitting? Or baking!

GIRLFRIEND: Ugh, knitting. I need a new hobby at my age? Grandmothers are supposed to be warm and compassionate and cuddly. Grandpas have no responsibilities. They don't have to tolerate children. They can make insensitive, off-colour remarks—and people think it's adorable. They can tell terrible jokes — I love terrible jokes! As a grandpa, I can play chess in the park in the middle of the afternoon. I can watch the old "dubya-dubya two" pictures on television.

BOYFRIEND: Well, you are kind of racist and you do love movies about Nazis.

GIRLFRIEND: I don't *love* the Nazis. I love pictures about *beating* the Nazis.

BOYFRIEND: Still, a lady grandfather? That's not how nature works. Don't you think it's a bit... privileged of you to self-identify in a masculine way. If you weren't a white woman, you wouldn't be able to pull this off.

GIRLFRIEND: How dare you! I'm blazing a trail for people of all kinds to be able to live openly as Grandpas.

BOYFRIEND: This is too weird.

GIRLFRIEND: If you can't handle this, I got a full bag of Werther's Originals and the boxset of *Matlock* at home, so... *(starts to leave)*

BOYFRIEND: No, it's not you. Well, it's you a little bit. I mean, I think it's great that you've found yourself. I'm not sure what role I've played in your discovery... it's just... this is not the first time a woman has had a personal identity awakening with me.

GIRLFRIEND: Oh yeah?

BOYFRIEND: Something about dating me triggers an epiphany about a woman's sense of self, I guess? My first girlfriend turned into a Mermaid. My girlfriend at university discovered she was a Juggalo. Another became a nudist... that wasn't so bad except she was sushi chef. The next one left me for one of her characters in The Sims game and married him last year... they just adopted Tamagotchi triplets. And my last girlfriend self-identified as a sloth — the animal not the sin.

GIRLFRIEND: They all sound adorable.

BOYFRIEND: What happened to normal women?!

GIRLFRIEND: That's not a thing.

BOYFRIEND: *(shrill)* Lady Grandpa isn't a thing!

GIRLFRIEND: Lemme tell you something—this culture is so obsessed with youth. Forty is the new twenty, sixty is the new middle-aged, and thirty-five is barely legal. "Adult" means something dirty and "Mature" means you're over the hill. No one wants to be old and yet our bodies continue to age. I'm watching the Generation X get gray and wrinkly and frail. My disaffected heroes are now afflicted with aches and pains, thinking about life insurance and walk-in tubs. The whole aging population gets lumped together under the zippy label "Zoomer" because no one can really retire and active 70-year-olds bristle at being called elderly. Where do I fit in? I'm gonna grow old before I'm allowed to grow up. I've gotta go buy my pants at Forever 21 to play along with society's charade and maintaining a facade of youth. I didn't like being a teenager the first time, why should I fight to hold onto a part of life that I don't identify with simply because society romanticizes it? In my day, old people were allowed to be old. They weren't relevant anymore, but they could sit down and wear loose-fitting pants and soak their teeth in peace. Look, I don't mean to fetishize the elderly. The inevitable deterioration of the human body is terrible and I'm in no rush to experience that. I just feel that the "grandpa" as a subculture has a lot more sartorial freedom and fewer societal expectations. By the time I am legitimately elderly, we'll be going to rave parties in the all-purpose room in the nursing home and watching Brett and Blaine pop wheelies on their Rascals. "Oh! Look how vibrant and active we all are! Age is just a number! Ignore the cracking of my crumbling bones — that just means I'm still alive!" Why does the grocery store sound like a night club?! We didn't start the fire but maybe we should consider putting it out soon because the smoke is clouding sensible thinking. Youth may well be wasted on the young but comfort is wasted on the old. I just want to wear my cardigans, watch my classic movies, and yell at a few clouds while I can enjoy it.

The couple sit in silence for a beat.

BOYFRIEND: Yep. you're a Grandpa, alright.

GIRLFRIEND: This is what I'm saying. Where's that leave us?

BOYFRIEND: Well, nothing's really changed has it?

GIRLFRIEND: Still me. Just a more comfortable me.

BOYFRIEND: I do want you to be comfortable. You know I've never really gone for the heavy eye make-up and the stilettos and the hair products. Nothing else is going to change? You're not gonna make me call you by some old-man name like Morty or Elmer?

GIRLFRIEND: Someday you'll be an old man, *Kyle*.

BOYFRIEND: Fair point.

GIRLFRIEND: *(pulls a hard candy out of the pocket of her cardigan and seductively unwraps it)* You wanna go back to my place and I'll read *The Princess Bride* to you again?

BOYFRIEND: Will there be kissing?

GIRLFRIEND: It's not inconceivable.

BOYFRIEND: As you wish.

GIRLFRIEND wordlessly offers the unwrapped candy to BOYFRIEND. He nods. She feeds him the candy and they smile contentedly.

END OF SCENE. BLACK OUT.

THE HEIRESS' HABIT

Katharine Drexel, heiress to the Drexel fortune and aspiring nun, discusses her vocation with her trusted advisor, Bishop James O'Connor. (historical fiction)

CAST:
KATE - Katharine Drexel - 29 years old, heiress to Drexel fortune and aspiring nun, looks pale and tired, despondent
JIM - Bishop James O'Connor - 64 years old, Irish descent, formerly a priest in Philadelphia

SETTING: Drexel manor, Philadelphia, 1887

KATE is in the midst of disinterestedly packing her steamer trunks. JIM enters.

JIM: Good morning, Kate!

KATE: Oh, hello, Your Excellency!

JIM: Must we always with the formalities? Please.

KATE: I was taught to demonstrate respect for my elders, Jim, you know that.

JIM: I do. My condolences for the loss of your father.

KATE: Thank you.

JIM: I regret that I was unable to attend his funeral. Frank was a fine and generous man and I was glad to call him friend for many years.

KATE: It would have pleased him to hear. You are feeling well now? What brings you back to the old stomping grounds?

JIM: I am attending to my brother, who himself is unwell.

KATE: I'm sorry. Seems to be going around.

KATE gestures for JIM to come sit.

KATE: I think Louise is making tea, if you'd like to join us.

JIM: I regret that I haven't long to stay.

KATE: Just a brief social call, then?

JIM: Aye.

KATE returns to her packing and sorting.

JIM: You're off to the old world, soon, are you?

KATE: My sisters thought a trip to Europe would boost our spirits. They've encouraged me to take a health cure at a mineral springs. It feels a bit indulgent.

JIM: You need your strength, Kate. You mustn't put spiritual health before physical health so much that you endanger both. If I may, you look as if you have seen better days.

KATE: Ah. The true intent for your visit. Did Lizzie send for you? Uncle Anthony?

JIM: Your letters of late have lacked your signature conviviality.

KATE: I confess that I am relieved to see you.

JIM: Are you unwell, my dear?

KATE: The future again looks vague and uncertain.

JIM: You've experienced the traumatic loss of both parents in a short time. Grief can often cloud the future's horizon.

KATE: Grief, yes, and guilt.

JIM: Whatever should you feel guilt for, Kate? Are you angry at God for taking your parents?

KATE: Not angry. I don't understand why He needed to take them so soon, but He has never given me cause for doubt. No, I am conflicted, Your Excellency, torn between my duty to my family and my commitment to the church.

JIM: 'Twas ever thus, my dear.

KATE: I feel more ready than ever to join the order and devote the rest of my life to the church. Despite carrying on with dear Mama's charity, it is hard to face the community that loved her so. They miss her beauty and grace, which I am sorely lacking. I know, I mustn't be vain.
Still, even in their gratitude, I can sense their disappointment when it is I who greets them.

JIM: Grief can colour our own perception of self worth. Surely the poor that you serve wish to extend their sorrow for your pain.

KATE: But there is something about receiving kindness from a beautiful soul who is also physically beautiful. Louise, being Mama's natural kin, should be face of the Drexel family — oh, but I just cannot burden and abandon her! I know she will do her best to serve, and Elizabeth, too. Even Papa, before he passed, was keen to keep up with Mama's charity and rent contributions to Philadelphia's poor single mothers. I worry, through all our best efforts, that history will overlook their kindnesses, Papa and Mama. History often neglects the kind-hearted. "Don't let the poor have cold feet," Mama said. I feel compelled to continue her works, and to take her teachings further — that we should reach out to our fellow man to give them the comfort we feel and which everyone deserves. Freely have you received; freely give.

JIM: Presumably your father's will prohibits you from freely giving it all at once.

KATE: Papa shrewdly protected us from those who would part us with his wealth, be it suitors or charities. However, even in death his generosity with his wealth continues without assistance from me or my sisters. We won't let the poor suffer, but, oh, how I long for peace far from the Drexel fortune. What am I to do, Jim?

JIM: May your travels bring comfort and illuminate the next phase of your spiritual journey. You needn't decide now on a religious or secular life. One can serve God with equal good will and devotion wherever He calls one.

KATE: You are still withholding your blessing for me to join the contemplative order then?

JIM: Many young people come to the church often believing they have been called, only to find some other purpose to lure them away. You still have your youth, beauty, wealth, social position, and a long life.

KATE: I'm hardly youthful anymore.

JIM: When you get to my age, my dear, everyone is young.

KATE: At nearly 30 and unmarried, I'm an old spinster by society's standards. The marriage question is posed only by fortune hunters and society vampires.

JIM: Your devotion to the calling is admirable. However —

KATE: We have discussed this ad nauseam. Shall I go into politics? Politics corrupt the soul. Philanthropy serves my fortune and family legacy but gives me no satisfaction in God's will being done.

JIM: What of your ambition, then?

KATE: I have no ambition.

JIM: Not to fame or leisure, but to aiding the poor and neglected. So long as you are a private citizen, you may do whatever you like with your resources. The sacrifices you would make in a convent… well, some are better suited to a quiet life of prayer and reflection.

KATE: So long as my contributions fall under the Drexel name, my motives will be suspect. A quiet life of prayer and reflection is what I need.

JIM: You are destined for bigger things, my dear. A bit more patience is what you need.

KATE: Does God estimate the greatness of human actions according to the work accomplished or according to the motives which induced the actions? I don't expect to be sainted but I would like to leave more behind than the Mary Katharine Drexel Library for Gifted Ladies.

JIM: Your sisters are accepting of your taking the vow?

KATE: Louise has remarked her surprise that I have not yet. She jokes that I'm already living by the vows of chastity and obedience — it is more truth than jest. The rest of our family disapproves — "Kate must be hysterical to trade her ball gowns for a nun's habit!" I've long given up ball gowns and high society! When Mama fell ill, I rejected countless invites to galas and soirees to sit at her bedside. She needed me more than I needed to squeeze into a whalebone corset to listen to another railroad baron claiming to be Benjamin Franklin's great-nephew. I didn't know how much that time with her would feel like a gift.

JIM: Playing nursemaid to your dying stepmother hardly seems like a gift.

KATE: I loved her dearly. All the money in the world couldn't buy effective cancer cures, but being with dear Mama through her prolonged illness and death strengthened my resolve. I know it is my duty to alleviate the suffering of as many people as possible.

JIM: Why not become a nurse?

KATE: I'm no Florence Nightingale. My friend Alice attended the new nursing school and works in the hospital. As often as she saves lives, she is subjected to proposals of marriage and fornication. That is not the vocation God would see fit for me.

JIM: A teacher then? You helped Lizzie build a couple of schools out west several summers ago. You could run your own Sunday school for infidels and savages.

KATE: *(horrified)* They are NOT ... those things!

JIM: When they were found, they were ululating naked around campfires. They haven't even the decency to defecate in private. Left to their own devices, Lord knows what they'll do.

KATE: I never thought you to be so cruel, Jim.

JIM: Everything we've done has improved their lives — we've given them food and clothing, taught them skills. If we can teach them the value of prayer, perhaps we can save those souls, but they'll never be much more than dressed-up animals.

KATE: *(becoming more impassioned)* Our people have tortured these poor souls. We've invaded tribal lands, we've abducted people from their home countries. We don't know the struggles they endured before our interference —

JIM: Getting trampled by bison, arm wrestling with tigers…

KATE: The Natives and the Negroes haven't chosen to live in this world. They've had their choices stolen from them.

JIM: The greater their sacrifice on Earth, the greater the reward in Heaven.

KATE: But they aren't like you or me, making the choice to heed God's calling to serve. Why must they be forced to endure suffering at the hands of their fellow man in order to recognize the rewards of the kingdom of Heaven?

JIM: The Lord determines in which laps to place luxury and on which shoulders to place burdens. What people do within their circumstances determines whether they earn their passage through the pearly gates. Who are we to question God's plan?

KATE: I cannot fathom that it is God's will for one human being to enslave another or to keep them in a subservient position. His children need protection, whatever form they take.

JIM: Consider it a test — the actions of those holding power and their distribution of wealth will show Him who is truly deserving and who has faltered.

KATE: The powerful have only faith in the almighty dollar and deem my family foolish for our charity. Sometimes I think these men to be demons sent to test my faith.

JIM: Aye, they do often resemble the Devil's disciples, sowing seeds of doubt and temptation. The church does impress upon them their duty to serve, imploring them to provide aid to the suffering.

KATE: What of my father? Has he passed the Lord's test?

JIM: Frank was a rare kind man who saw the benefit in charity. He was fortunate to be blessed with compassionate women to keep him steady on his path.

KATE: He saw potential in the Natives and Negros. He funded the schools out west, to help tribes acclimate to the changes happening around them.

JIM: 'Tis a noble pursuit to tame the wild man.

KATE: Where is your faith where men of colour are concerned? These are not "dressed-up animals" to be tamed! Louise and I were discussing the freeing of Negro slaves and how much adversity they've faced and the courage they've displayed through it all — what is my grief compared to the horrors they've experienced? My God, they are the very picture of the triumph of the human spirit. I can see no one more deserving of our love and compassion than those who have suffered so needlessly as the Native tribes and the enslaved. It should be our mission to serve them and aid them as they aim to participate in society as whole, free people.

JIM: In a just world…

KATE: It is our duty to make it a just world. But money simply isn't enough! We need missionaries to bring hope and empathy, not only food and Bibles. With positive encouragement, the Indian and Black peoples could make tremendous improvements to a society into which they've been unfairly thrust.

JIM: Kate —

KATE: And if we leave it in the hands of the powerful to attend to the poor, will they not simply offer just enough to placate? We need to elevate the poor…

JIM: Katharine!

KATE: What?! *(surprised at herself)* Oh.

JIM: Is it wise for you to be so stimulated in your weakened condition?

KATE: I am feeling a bit flushed. Social injustice raises my ire.

JIM: No one could dare question your faith in those people. It is that passion that will serve you well in the church.

KATE: …I have your blessing?

JIM: My child, you've always had my blessing!

KATE: If that were true, why have you have persuaded me so fervently and with such frequency to not join the order?

JIM: Your father insisted that I advise you against joining an order so early in your life. He even built it into earlier drafts of his will to never permit you to enter a convent until you were at least 25 years of age.

KATE: Papa forbid me from becoming a nun? He never made mention of this to me.

JIM: He was concerned that you romanticized the idea of becoming a nun, without understanding the sacrifices that cloistered sisters make. He recalled your excitement joining your mother for visits with her sister Madame Louise at her convent, and how eager you were to take vows. Frank believed you were clinging to the notion of a religious life to avoid beaus — or the absence of beaus.

KATE: I was perhaps a vain girl. But my devotion to the church is entirely separate from my interest in taking a husband. What counsel do you have for me now?

JIM: Are you not troubled to learn that your father kept you from your calling?

KATE: I know how Papa valued our family and I cherish all the moments we had together. I trust that Papa and the Lord kept me on the virtuous path. And receiving your blessing lifts such a weight from my heart. *(excitedly)* What am I to do now? Shall I join the Convent of the Sacred Heart? Would Aunt Lou accept me or is that akin to nepotism since she was Mama's biological sister?

JIM: Slow down, child! Attend to your travels, first. Be with your biological sisters before racing into the sisterhood — which I still do not advise.

KATE: But —

JIM: To join a contemplative order such as Sacred Heart, you would be asked to surrender all that is yours, including your missionary work. You're best suited for one of the apostolic orders, after your noviciate, of course.

KATE: Then I should join an apostolic order, one dedicated to serving Native tribes and Negro communities.

JIM: There is no such order. But — oh! Of course! You should found your own order.

KATE: My own order? Me, Mother Katharine? That is many years off, even if I started my noviciate today —

JIM: We could begin as soon as you complete your noviciate. All you need is a bishop's approval to back your mission, so long as that mission fills a unique need. Bishop James O'Connor at your service.

KATE: But if you believe the Negroes and Native people to be inferior, will you not compromise my mission?

JIM: I believe in you, Kate. If anyone could bring those people closer to salvation, in whatever form it may come, it is you. I can see now you're meant to harness the power of the church for the greater good.

KATE: My head is spinning. I've not felt this much elation in, well, years!

JIM: Sit, my dear girl, sit.

KATE sits. KATE then excitedly kneels to pray, but quickly returns to the chair.

KATE: What about the Pope? Do I need his blessing?

JIM: If anyone could get the Pope's blessing, it's our industrious Katharine Drexel.

KATE: Thank you, your excellency! Oh, I must tell Louise! Where is she with the tea?

JIM rises and KATE bounces up to embrace him.

JIM: I must be on my way in any case. Enjoy your travels and be well, my dear. In the meantime, I'll see to it to send a few missionary priests out West. When you return from Europe, big things will be set in motion!

KATE: Thank you, Jim! God bless you!

JIM exits. KATE, in a state of excitement, starts to pray again, moves to return to her trunk, then moves to exit to the kitchen.

KATE: *(calling off-stage)* Louise! You'll never believe it — I'm going to be a mother!

END OF SCENE. BLACK OUT.

INCESTRY DOT COM

A mother and daughter discuss their family history in the Deep South.

CAST:
MAMA - 60+ woman, lower class with a deep Southern drawl, wears a faded house dress and cheap slippers
BABY MAE - 45 year old woman, dressed a little smarter but also speaks with a deep Southern drawl that betrays her middle class appearance

SETTING: On a wraparound porch of a family farmhouse in rural Alabama, summertime

On a sweltering early August evening, the two women sit in rocking chairs and sip iced tea from mason jars.

MAMA: Lawdy, but it's hot!

BABY MAE: Yes'm.

MAMA: I don't reckon it's been this hot in a mighty long while.

BABY MAE: Weatherman Ron said it's gon' stay hot for the foreseeable.

MAMA: You'd think it'd cool off once the sun sets, but it jus' don't do that way anymore.

BABY MAE: Lots of things ain't like they used to be.

MAMA: Go tell that, Baby Mae.

BABY MAE: Hey, Mama.

MAMA: Yea'huh?

BABY MAE: I'm fixin' to be 45 in a little bit.

MAMA: Mmhmm.

BABY MAE: Ain't it about time to change my given name from "Baby Mae"?

MAMA: But you are still my little Baby Mae.

BABY MAE: It's jus' real hard to be taken seriously at work. Cain't I just be Mae now?

MAMA: Then how we gon' tell you apart from Mammy Mae?

BABY MAE: Well, Mammy Mae's up in heaven and I'm here.

MAMA: We still gots to pray for both of ya. Besides, you done okay for yourself up to now. And "Judge Baby Mae Williams" sounds real good in that courtroom. Your cousins' been real proud to have you presidin' over their bail hearin's and whatnot.

BABY MAE: It's come to my attention that most of them boys ain't real cousins.

MAMA: We all god's children and we all related in some way.

BABY MAE: Even the monkeys?

MAMA: Only cousin Michael.

They rock in their chairs and fan themselves.

BABY MAE: Lawdy, it's hot!

MAMA: I cain't think straight.

BABY MAE: Maybe if we don't think about it, it'll be more tolerable.

MAMA: Alright. Why don't you tell me what's been goin' on with you baby girl?

BABY MAE: Oh! I tried goin' online to look up our ancestry for granny's birthday, 'cause I heard you can do a search and find out iffen you're related to famous people and thought she'd get a kick out of learnin' we're related to Robert E. Lee or Paula Deen or somethin', but I ain't found much on us yet.

MAMA: Well, we ain't much for bein' online, since your brother got in trouble with the law for lookin' at all them pictures of nekkid girls.

BABY MAE: Online don't really work that way, Mama. What I did was I put granddaddy's name into the ancestry site but there was too many Willie Johnsons. And a surprisin' number of them had daddies named Ezekiel Johnson. I don't suppose you got more specific details I could use, like where was they all born and who came over from the U.K. and such?

MAMA: *(sighs)* You know, you a real smart girl, Baby Mae. I don't know how you ain't figure this stuff out all on your own yet.

BABY MAE: What stuff?

MAMA: Your daddy ain't being your real daddy, for one.

BABY MAE: Lord knows he sure done behaved enough like he ain't my daddy. But wait, who is my real daddy then?

MAMA: Your uncle.

BABY MAE: *(horrified)* Your brother?

MAMA: *(scoffs)* No. Your daddy's brother.

BABY MAE: My uncle's brother?

MAMA: Your uncle's brother is really your uncle. And his brother is really your daddy.

BABY MAE: That's not confusin' at all! But granddaddy is still my granddaddy?

MAMA: Yes'm. That is, if your granny's telling the truth. She got around with a buncha fellers in her day. Your granddaddy, the pastor's son, a whole mess o' army boys durin' the war, my daddy, the milk man, the paper boy, and she was real friendly with them fellers in the traveling circus. You got to understand that was a different time, Baby Mae. A girl could court several beaus 'till one of 'em had to marry 'er.

BABY MAE sips on tea and mulls over this new information.

BABY MAE: Mama?

MAMA: Yeah.

BABY MAE: You mean to tell me you were with my daddy and my uncle-daddy?

MAMA: Well… no.

BABY MAE: So, my sisters are my sisters or my cousins?

MAMA: They are your sisters in the ways that count.

BABY MAE: Mama… are you really my Mama?

MAMA: I'm as real a Mama as you need.

BABY MAE: You ain't givin' me real satisfyin' answers here.

MAMA: Well, you know your big sister?

BABY MAE: Margie or Girleen?

MAMA: Margie.

BABY MAE: Yes, I believe we have made acquaintance.

MAMA: Well, she had a dalliance with your uncle-daddy one time and didn't tell nobody 'til you come out.

BABY MAE: So... my sister is my mother and my uncle is my daddy? And that makes you really my grandmother?

MAMA: If you want to look at it biologickly, then, yes.

BABY MAE: This is one mangled family tree.

MAMA: I don't think we got but the one branch.

They sit quietly, continuing to sip tea and fan themselves.

BABY MAE: Gotdang, it's hot!

MAMA: Watch your mouth! You ain't too big for a switch.

BABY MAE: Mama? *(scoffs and rolls her eyes)* Mama.

MAMA: Yes, Baby Mae.

BABY MAE: I jus' don't know what to make of all this. What do you reckon I should do?

MAMA: Most of us take to the drink or the bible. Sometimes both. A hollered-out bible makes a good hidey-hole for a flask.

BABY MAE: Bless y'all's hearts.

MAMA: Lawdy, it's hot! Baby, go fix us some more sweet tea.

BABY MAE: Yes'm.

MAMA: And bring us my goin' to meetin' bible. We'll do a little studyin' from the gospel of Jack Daniels.

BABY MAE: Yes'm!

BABY MAE takes both mason jars and exits. MAMA rocks in her chair and hums "(Give Me That) Old-Time Religion".

END OF SCENE. BLACK OUT.

THE LEGEND OF S

A professor delivers a lecture on the origin of a mysterious symbol. Over the course of his lecture, he compulsively draws more and more of the symbol on available media and surfaces.

<u>CAST:</u>
PROFESSOR - late 30s/early 40s, dressed in pyjamas with a tweedy blazer/ sports coat and tortoiseshell glasses, which he is constantly trying to push back up his nose, regardless of actual slippage.
SECURITY GUARD - 40s-50s, blue collar, gruff but sympathetic. he's encountered the professor giving previous lectures before.

PROFESSOR enters with a stack of papers and books, sets them on the table. He looks out to the audience and studies them briefly, pushes glasses up on nose. After a moment, he goes to chalkboard (or whiteboard) and draws the pointy S on a chalkboard.

(Alternatively, after sizing up the audience, he pulls a folded piece of paper out of his pocket, unfolds it and holds it up with the Pointy S drawing facing outward towards the audience.)

PROFESSOR: Can anyone tell me what this is? Anyone? No one? *(takes place behind lectern and bangs his fist on the top)* Nobody knows! Despite decades, if not centuries of its existence, it seems no one on the face of the Earth knows what this symbol is, where it came from, or what it means. No human throughout history has been willing to take credit for the invention of this… pointy S-like thing that inexplicably manifests itself on school notebooks, washroom stalls and garage doors. No one knows how it came to be scrawled large across faded billboards for menthol cigarettes and carved deep into wooden railings of remote parklands. I recall my days as a young lad, joining fellow classmates in idly sketching this very shape in the margins of our composition books. We hadn't a clue where it came from, but it looked cool, so we decorated book covers and binders with it for years until, one day… we didn't. As mysteriously as it entered our prepubescent lives, it vanished from our doodle repertoire and our minds. A few months ago, the memories came rushing back when I spied Kevin, my nine-year-old nephew drawing on the cover of his notebook the same Pointy S that I'd done 30-odd years before. My curiosity piqued, I inquired where he'd gotten the notion to draw it. He responded with a most eloquent "dunnuh." Well! As the adjunct Professor of Arcane Marginalia at the University of Margaritaville, I couldn't let this mystifying matter drop. I've spent countless hours poring over historic tomes, reviewing ancient symbols and alphabets, even scanning design manuals for branded word-marks that might match this character. I've interrogated fellow colleagues and former classmates. I've consulted experts—historians, typographers, mathematicians, and psychic advisors. I've scoured the internet, reading dozens of articles and message boards and countless Subreddits. My findings have revealed that while everyone recognizes the doodle itself and confesses to copying it onto their own notebooks between the ages of eight and eleven, they haven't any clue about its origins. With no recorded historical significance and no documented point of origin, it's as if the proliferation of pointy esses emblazoned on edifices was perpetrated by stealthy, street-tough fairies with gossamer wings and leather jackets, armed with spray paint and jackknives, working under cover of night to spread their mysterious message for children to see on their commute to school, with no discernible purpose than to serve as an unspoken tradition passed on through schoolchildren, regardless of gender, class, or nationality. At this moment, young Martians and Venusians could be doodling it in their notebook margins alongside crude drawings of old Mrs. Jefferson with a large quantity of stink lines emitting from her bottom. Those lacking curiosity reckon the Pointy S is an asemic morpheme, a simple doodle, merely an alternative to your run-of-the-mill cube, requiring no skill or thought for mindless doodling during boring lectures or while on hold with customer service, so, of course it's attractive to children and I'm overthinking things again and this is why I'll never find love. Excuse me for being intrigued by what is possibly the greatest phenomenon of the 20th century, Marsha! *(scribbling on paper or whiteboard as he speaks)* Look, most doodles can be identified.

Here's a square. Oh, look, now it's a cube. Here's a circle. Now it's a smiley face. Now it's Mr. Sunshine piercing heat rays into some nearby clouds. Here's some doodly little hearts for the girls out there. Let's add some stars here… oooh, shooting stars. Ah! Here's Mr. Chad to tell us "Kilroy was here." *(holds up a detailed drawing of an alien)* Here's Zorbert, an intergalactic acquaintance of mine who comes round to get me into or out of harebrained schemes. *(draws a bunch of arrows pointing to the other doodles)* We've got easily identifiable doodles coming out of our yin yangs! *(draws a yin yang)* But this — *(gestures to the pointy S he drew)* A profane hieroglyphic? Rogue Aztec graffiti? A symbol for an abandoned form of currency? A doodle from da Vinci's discarded bar napkin? Sure, it's easy to do — just draw two equidistant sets of three parallel lines, then join them diagonally from left to right, and cap off at the top and bottom with pointy bits. Put it all together and what've you got? A Pointy S. But why? And why does it mostly appeal to young children for such a brief window of time? A lot of people presume the Pointy S is inspired by a logo from a popular heavy metal band or superhero or skateboard company. These presumptions can be easily debunked with a simple side-by-side comparison of the S to these logos. Then, for every six suppositions that the Pointy S is some sort of logo, one person counters that it must be a gang sign, a theory loosely based on a lone observation of the symbol tucked amongst some roadside graffiti and the notion that all graffiti must be gang-related. This theory was cooked up by authority figures always keen to attribute things they don't understand to gangs. For years, apparently, the Pointy S has been misattributed to the Stüssy brand. So prevalent is this myth that the Pointy S is generally identified by the misnomer Stüssy S. *(holds up a print out of the Stüssy logos)* However, a simple web image search brings up the official Stüssy logo in its variations since the company's formation in the 1980s and not one is identical to the Pointy S. Despite this contrary evidence, a surprising majority of people who correspond on Internet forums are willing to blithely accept this and go about their lives. "Close enough," they say. I say even if you justify that the Pointy S is based in part on this one particular S, you still haven't rationalized why it is pointy on either end.

(leans in close over his stack of books) Now, there is one plausible theory suggesting this symbol originated as a puzzle in a 1950s issue of Scholastic magazine, one of those teasers — "use these six lines to draw an S". Of course, there is no recorded evidence of this mid-century ephemera and the question remains—where did this variation of the letter S originate? Who, in 1950s America, was drawing esses with straight lines? When the modern S had been beautifully simplified to one smooth curvy line, who's mission was it to make it so very complex and pointy? My colleague in the university's Pseudohistory department theorizes the symbol was first observed in the margins of the 1965 edition of a Harcourt Brace science textbook, put forth as part of a grand experiment in unconscious perception by the textbook publisher and used in conjunction with subliminal messaging inserted into educational filmstrips. The experiment was designed to measure how susceptible students were to subliminal stimuli and their response. For example, would students subjected to a viewing of The History of Science pick up on suggestive messages to doodle the Pointy S whilst learning how Benjamin Franklin invented the steam-powered toaster? Eventually, my colleague surmises, the Pointy S was adopted independent of Harcourt Brace and was passed on organically by students via textbooks and any surface onto which a child could make a tiny mark of rebellion. We may never know the true progenitor of the Pointy S. Many of you will return to your homes tonight, satisfied to believe the disproved explanation that the Pointy S is the Stüssy logo. "Meh, works for me," you'll say to your spouse. "Banksy probably added those pointy bits to make a creative statement. That professor was clearly mad for suggesting it could be anything else. Marsha was right to kick him out. Why would anyone dedicate their lives to examining the minutiae of Marginalia anyway? They're just doodles for fuck's sake! Starving children in Africa don't even have the strength to draw circles in the sand, much less esses of any angularity." Well, why are you so willing to accept easily debunked theories?! You could have so much fun devising your own outlandish theories and posting them to the Internet. My own theory starts in the margins, where the Pointy S is typically found, first discovered as a drollery lifted from an ancient

illuminated manuscript, the handiwork of a sneaky 11-year-old monk's apprentice making reference to the popular Medieval rune-based card game Crazy Aetts. In its original form, the Pointy S was turned horizontally, resembling a sort of rustic infinity symbol. It was turned to its more recognizable vertical aspect when adapted for Lord Cumberland Lovelady's North Sherbetshire League of Vagrants in the late 18th century. Ooh! Another possibility could be a rudimentary take on the section sign (§), that obscure yet ubiquitous symbol scattered about in legal documents.

The PROFESSOR goes to his stack of books, picks one out of the middle of the stack and begins thumbing through it.

PROFESSOR: If I could refer you to section 7 of Kevin's grade three mathematics textbook, I think you'll find the Pointy S—

SECURITY GUARD enters.

SECURITY GUARD: Alright, Professor, time to go.

PROFESSOR: But I was giving a lecture to these people—

SECURITY GUARD: You sure were, buddy. Come on.

SECURITY GUARD moves to guide PROFESSOR away.

PROFESSOR: All of my theories— And the pointy-ness—

SECURITY GUARD: Yeah, yeah. *(notices all the esses drawn by the professor)* Say, that's the Stüssy logo, ain't it? We used to draw that at school. Ha!

PROFESSOR whimpers and sobs as he's escorted away.

END OF SCENE. BLACK OUT.

MILESTONES

Harry's in for a big birthday surprise when he finds his wife and best friend in bed together.

CAST:
HARRY - (40s) *fully clothed except barefoot*
JENNIFER - (30s-40s) *HARRY's wife, in a state of undress*
STEVE - (30s-40s) *HARRY's best friend and JENNIFER's lover, in a state of undress*

SETTING: *A domestic bedroom*

HARRY walks into a bedroom, where romantic accoutrements are scattered about and JENNIFER and STEVE are in bed together. HARRY opens a dresser drawer and retrieves a pair of socks.

JENNIFER notices HARRY's entrance and gasps. STEVE and JENNIFER, embarrassed, scramble to disentangle themselves and cover up.

JENNIFER: Harry!

HARRY: Oh, hi guys. Don't mind me. Just getting a pair of socks.

STEVE: *You* don't mind?

HARRY: Why should I?

STEVE: This must look terrible. Catching us like this?

HARRY: No need to cover up. I'm onto you.

JENNIFER: You could be more upset.

HARRY: Ah. Right. *(mock gasps)* Oh, no! My wife and my best friend? How could you do this to me? *(chuckles)*

JENNIFER: You're taking this surprisingly well.

HARRY: C'mon, I know what you guys are really up to.

STEVE: What do you think we're up to?

HARRY sits down to put on his socks.

HARRY: Really? The sneaking around, the furtive glances and whispers, the secret phone calls? Jennifer at her book club and Steve going bowling? Jennifer hate book clubs and Steve hasn't gone bowling since throwing his back out two years ago. Plus, you're always asking what my plans are to make sure I'm out of the way, there's the big hotel charge on the credit card bill — It's so obvious that you're planning my birthday party.

JENNIFER: What?

STEVE: Huh?

JENNIFER: Harry —

HARRY: I'm sorry. I've spoiled the surprise!

JENNIFER: No, Harry, you've got it all wrong.

HARRY: It's no use hiding it any longer.

JENNIFER: We're not planning a party for you.

HARRY: Riiiiiiiiight.

STEVE: Seriously, Harry.

JENNIFER: Steve and I — we've been having an affair.

STEVE: For almost a year.

HARRY: You guys are determined to keep this up.

JENNIFER: We're being honest with you now, Harry. I'm sorry this is how you had to find out.

STEVE: Frankly, I forgot your birthday was coming up.
(to JENNIFER) I was so focused on plans for our anniversary next week.

HARRY: *(disbelieving)* So, the hotel — was not for the ballroom rental?

JENNIFER: No, Harry.

STEVE: It was the penthouse suite — for Jennifer and me.

JENNIFER: *(to STEVE)* To celebrate…?

STEVE: *(to JENNIFER)* Our first year together!

HARRY: Really? *First*? Year? Together! …Well, congratulations!

STEVE: Harry —

JENNIFER: Harry, please.

HARRY: This is just great.

JENNIFER: We didn't want you to find out this way.

HARRY: Just super — fantastic!

HARRY paces around the room while JENNIFER and STEVE get dressed and out of bed.

HARRY: *(pulls a credit card statement out of his pocket)* So, the floral arrangements, the boxes of chocolate, the lingerie, the very expensive scotch, the holiday in Barbados... none of that is for me, for my birthday?

JENNIFER: No.

STEVE: How'd you get my credit card statements?

HARRY: My wife and my best friend are celebrating their first of what sounds like many years of an affair behind my back and they ruined my 40th birthday.

STEVE: *(picks up the scotch and presents it to HARRY)* You can have the scotch, if you like.

HARRY: I do not like! *(snatches the bottle from STEVE and looks at the label)* Actually, I like very much. *(turns back to STEVE)* But you — how dare you?

STEVE: Me? What about you?

JENNIFER: Guys! This is not the time.

HARRY: Not the time for what, darling? To talk about the fact that my marriage is in shambles, my career is over, my whole life has been a lie, and all my dreams are dead —

STEVE: You're overreacting.

HARRY: Am I, Steve?!

STEVE: Be honest, what are you more upset about right now, the fact that Jennifer and I are in love or that we forgot your birthday?

JENNIFER: I didn't forget, Harry. I just didn't plan anything.

HARRY: Jesus!

STEVE: Well?

HARRY: I mean, my 40th birthday! That's a milestone, something worth commemorating, the prime of my life. Top of the hill, baby! It's all down hill from there. Over the hill, that's where I'm headed. Over the hill and past my prime, out of work and all alone. What am I gonna do? Where am I gonna go? Who's going to love a rotten wretch like me now, Jennifer?

JENNIFER: I'm sorry, Harry. But, you know, 40 is the new 25 these days. Getting older isn't as bad as it used to be.

HARRY: Tell it to my back and my knees and my hairline and my waistline. Twenty-five year olds don't get a backache from standing in line at the grocery store.

JENNIFER: So, you're a little out of shape.

HARRY: I'm running out of time!

HARRY opens the bottle of scotch and starts chugging it. STEVE wrestles the bottle away from HARRY.

STEVE: Whoa, Harry! Slow down there.

HARRY: What's the use?

STEVE: Maybe we ought to do something, Jennifer. *(to HARRY)* Look, I'll round up some of the guys, we'll hit a couple of pubs, and drink to the next 40 years.

HARRY: Just park me outside the liquor store and I'll drink away the next 40 years.

STEVE: We can't leave you alone now, can we?

HARRY: Why not? That's the plan eventually, right? Leave ol' Harry alone, friendless, loveless, jobless, and homeless.

JENNIFER: Hold on — Harry, you lost your job?

HARRY: Oh, didn't I tell you? I was fired from the video store yesterday. Twenty years with Tony's Dry Clean and Video. Tony's son decides he's dropping the videos to expand the dry cleaning division.

JENNIFER: To be fair, this has been a long time coming, right?

HARRY: I dedicated the best years of my life to the film industry and this is how it treats me.

STEVE: Renting video tapes to people who're dropping off their dry cleaning isn't really part of the film industry.

HARRY: Important people have their clothes dry cleaned, Steve. A Hollywood bigwig could've come in at any time to get a suit cleaned and I could've slipped him my screenplay. Now *Clean Getaway* will never get made.

JENNIFER: You waited twenty years for a chance meeting with a movie executive? Renting video tapes to elderly people in Brampton?

HARRY: And now that chance will never come.

JENNIFER: Oh, Harry.

HARRY: What do I do? Where do I go now?

JENNIFER: You can stay here as long as you need. I can stay at Steve's.

HARRY: Me, stay here? In our marital home? And sleep in our marital bed which you have defiled?

JENNIFER: I'm sorry, Harry. It's not like we planned this.

STEVE: We did plan some of this.

HARRY snatches the scotch back from STEVE and starts to leave.

HARRY: *(to bottle)* My real friend and I are going to find someplace quiet to enjoy each other's company.

JENNIFER: Take the hotel! *(to STEVE)* It's the least we can do, Steve. *(to HARRY)* Take our suite at the hotel. For tonight. It is your birthday, after all.

HARRY: Oh, okay… thanks.

STEVE: And think of all of this as an opportunity.

HARRY: The total destruction and utter collapse of my life is an opportunity?

JENNIFER: Yes! Use this as a launch pad to achieve your dreams.

HARRY: But our life here —

JENNIFER: Don't you see, I was holding you back! Now you're free to move to Hollywood and pitch your screenplay out there.

HARRY: Pfft. What're the odds I'll find a job at another dry clean slash video store?

JENNIFER: You could… look for a job at a place that just sells videos.

HARRY: I only know how to rent videos, Jennifer.

JENNIFER: You don't have to figure it all out right this minute.

HARRY: That's it then? You two are in love and I'm out of luck.

JENNIFER: Nobody said anything about love.

HARRY: Steve did, earlier.

JENNIFER: Oh. *(to STEVE)* You mean it?

STEVE: Of course. Look at all the plans I made. That's not for nothing.

JENNIFER: Oh, Steve!

JENNIFER and STEVE embrace and kiss passionately.

HARRY: *(sarcastically)* So glad to be here for this moment.

STEVE and JENNIFER remember their embarrassment and pull away.

STEVE: I'm sorry about all this, Harry. Tell you what — you take the trip to Barbados.

JENNIFER gasps and scoffs.

STEVE: *(to JENNIFER)* We did destroy this guy's life, babe.
(to HARRY) Okay, you remember my sister Belinda?

HARRY: Belinda? Belinda! I had such a crush on her in college.

STEVE: She was just telling me how she has a crush on you and couldn't believe Jennifer would treat you this way. *(looks to JENNIFER and mouths "Sorry")* I was gonna set you two up eventually, after, you know, we told you about this.

HARRY: Wow. Wow! Really? Really!

STEVE: You and Belinda could spend a week in Barbados. And when you get back, you'll be refreshed and invigorated and ready to jump into the rest of your life.

HARRY: *(to JENNIFER)* You'd be okay with this?

JENNIFER: Go, with my blessing.

HARRY: You're so great, Jennifer. Except for the whole "cheating on me with my best friend" thing. Such a shame we couldn't make it work.

JENNIFER: *(deadpan)* Such a shame.

HARRY finds a box of chocolates on the bed and starts picking through to find a piece.

HARRY: Huh. A bottle of scotch, a night in the penthouse suite, a free trip to Barbados with my dream girl — no offense, Jennifer, and a chance to become a famous Hollywood screenwriter. Not so bad for a guy turning 41.

JENNIFER: 40.

HARRY: 41.

JENNIFER: You were just upset that we weren't throwing you a 40th birthday party.

HARRY: *(pops a chocolate piece in his mouth, speaks with his mouth full)* Ah. See, I thought maybe you guys might finally feel guilty — y'know, for bailing on me right before my 40th birthday last year to start your dirty affair, and for doing such a crap job of hiding your ongoing sexcapades — that you'd make it up to me this year with a big party. All this, though, is way better than that. Thanks, guys! *(grabs the scotch bottle and toasts the couple)* By the way — Happy anniversary! *(takes a big swig from the bottle)*

END OF SCENE. BLACK OUT.

MYSTERY SOLVED

Lord Roland Butterfield-Jones solves a most pressing mystery.

<u>CAST:</u>
LORD ROLAND BUTTERFIELD-JONES OF HRMSFORTH - *a distinguished gentleman of an advanced age, dressed for dinner but with a smoking jacket instead of formal dinner jacket, wielding a pipe*

SETTING: *The parlour of a posh manor, 1930s*

LORD ROLAND BUTTERFIELD-JONES *enters the parlour to address a room full of "suspects" for a mysterious revelation.*

LORD ROLAND: I suppose you're wondering why I have gathered you here tonight. A great mystery has occurred and we must get to the bottom of it! After dinner I was feeling quite agitated and supposed that a refreshing evening drive might alleviate some of my gastrointestinal distress. I went to the foyer to retrieve the keys to my roadster, only to see an empty key hook and my own dour reflection in the hall mirror. Who could've taken my keys? My car?! I dashed out to the garage at once to find my sporty coupe safely ensconced. A curious matter — Who would want my keys but not my coupe? As you are aware, preparations for Lady Agatha's bi-monthly formal gala — the one that clutters our main hall with the who's who of Whozzatshire — have caused quite a ruckus, with visitors swarming and flitting about and tradesmen traipsing through the house readying for tomorrow evening. Every caller entered through the main foyer and any one of them could have absconded with my key fob at any moment. But who had the motive? Which, if any, of these interlopers had incentive to commit Grand Theft Automobile Keys? Shall we review the goings-on of the day to suss out our key suspect? Let's see… the party planner met with Lady Agatha early this morning to finalize details for tomorrow's do. Then the decorator arrived to consult with Lady Agatha on wallpaper samples for the secret passages. Neither displayed any interest in motorcars. I observed little Roland Jr. here occupying himself with a set of jingling keys whilst plopped in the middle of the floor of the solarium. When I inquired after them, our butler, Thinman claimed ownership and responsibility as he'd lent his pantry keys to the tot in an effort to quiet him during one of Lady Agatha's headaches. Now, it's possible Roland, Jr. toddled his way into the foyer, found himself mesmerized by my keys up on their hook, climbed the antique coat rack, and snatched them down. A most unlikely scenario. Hrm… Dear Lady Agatha retired upstairs some hours ago with another headache and hasn't been seen since. Even the arrival of her latest acquisition could not rouse her from her bedchamber — what was it — a cricket diamond? The snooker sapphire? Baseball tiara? Apparently something that warrants throwing a party on a Wednesday night. Her maid has been skittering up and down the stairs, fetching all manners of ointments and concoctions for her. I suppose she could have borrowed my keys at the behest of Lady Agatha, though for reasons I cannot fathom. Sir Waggleston, the renowned kleptomaniac, has often been discovered transporting treasures to his underground lair in the garden. At the time in question, however, he was relentlessly hounding the nanny. *(bends to address dog in baby talk)* Weren't you, Sir Waggleston? Yes, you were. Yes, you were, my wittle snausage! Erf! *(clears throat, straightens posture)* Where was I? Ah! right. Now, the obvious suspect is my daughter Margaret, who came to me earlier in the day with a breathless desire to go driving, claiming it was a matter of life and death. Hmph, the death of my automobile most likely! I put the kibosh on that. She seemed quite anxious to get away — no doubt to see that lawyer chap who's been courting her with his vulgar Latin poetry, that Don Juan, Esquire. Come to think of it, she wasn't at dinner… Pfft! Probably still sulking, as young girls do. So, after that burst of drama, the locksmith came round to upgrade the locks on all the doors. Our last group of overnight guests complained about the large gaping keyholes into which wandering peepers could mosey. Before I could escort him upstairs, the carpet man arrived to steam the Persians and air out the Orientals. He was followed closely by the party planner, who returned to inquire about the RSVPs from esteemed invitees. As I was about to direct her upstairs to Lady Agatha's room, she had the audacity to ask whether

I would be fetching the prime minister from the aeroport before the event. Hmph! The PM can get his own ruddy ride from the aeroport for what we're paying him! He'll likely be boasting again about how he got his hands on the Duchess of Teacosy-upon-Noggin's newly augmented bust. He's storing the emerald-encrusted effigy at his flat next door until it can be presented at her birthday gala next week — thankfully not being hosted here! Speaking of my dearest neighbour, the plumbers were summoned to the cellar for emergency repair on the crumbling clay sewer pipes that lay betwixt our manors. The PM is forever moaning about the crumbling pipes of democracy backing up the flow of progress. The irony would be delightful if it weren't so inconvenient. Anyhow, I was on my way to investigate the situation, when the carpet man and locksmith descended the stairs with a lumpy, rolled up rug that I recognized from Margaret's room. The rug man claimed Lady Agatha was sending it away for mending and so I sent them away. As Thinman and I tried to steady ourselves from the whirling hubbub, an estate agent called Mitzi wandered in unannounced. She just happens to be selling a comparable property down the lane and asked for a tour of ours. I led the charming agent through the rooms as we chatted about tomorrow's event and all of today's commotion, housing prices — it's astounding what properties sell for these days! Maybe I can convince Lady Agatha to downsize if she ever tires of throwing these lavish parties. Well, with all this activity, it's no wonder dinner turned my stomach into a dance hall! After I discovered that my keys had vanished from the foyer, suddenly, the electricity went out! I heard three screams, including my own, followed by an eerie silence. I groped around for a torch and, upon finding one, started to make my way towards the cellar. While fumbling for the fuse box, I felt a sharp pain in my lower rib cage and fell to the floor. It was then I discovered that the key to my automobile had been in the left pocket of my waistcoat this entire time! Ha! Can you believe it? Oh, of all the things. Wait 'til I tell Aggie about this.

LORD ROLAND BUTTERFIELD-JONES *puffs on pipe and wanders away.*

END OF SCENE. BLACK OUT.

PHILOSOPHR 2.0

A millennial philosopher recounts a litany of nonsensical calamities.

CAST:
PHILOSOPHR - *Professorial with a space age beatnik flair.*

SETTING: *A bare stage with only a lectern or podium.*

The PHILOSOPHR enters and takes their place behind a lectern or podium and addresses the audience at large.

PHILOSOPHR: *(compassionately)* Hiya, friend. You say you lost your job today and all your side hustles went bust and it's only 9:45 in the morning and your phone battery is at 23% because your charger cord is dead and it's the third replacement you've bought this month? You say your avocado is half rotten and the pit is lodged pretty deep into the half that's still good and your gluten-free toast is burnt? You say someone in your building keeps taking your Amazon packages so you've placed the same order for shampoo and double-A batteries five times while your dandruff flakes all over your pillow and your smoke alarm goes off every 25 seconds and you can't reach the ceiling to change the batteries because your boyfriend stole your stepladder when he left last month to move in with a girl he met through a Google document? Is that what's troublin' you, bunky?

Cymbals crash and a brassy rendition of "National Emblem" plays.

PHILOSOPHR: *(boisterously)* Raise your blanket over your head and take a nap for awhile! You deserve some rest and self-care is important! Keep calm and try again tomorrow!

The music stops.

PHILOSOPHR: *(compassionately)* How ya doin', fella? You say there was another mass murder committed by a white man and you tried calling your senator about it but he was out hunting with an international oil tycoon? You say you went to the doctor for a cough and he wrote you a prescription but when you got to the pharmacy, they only had brand name capsules and your drug plan just covers generic? You say your rent keeps rising and so do the oceans and all your mutual acquaintances muted you on Twitter and you just cracked the screen on your smartphone the day after the warranty expired?
Is that what's on your mind, sport?

Cymbals crash and a brassy rendition of "National Emblem" plays.

PHILOSOPHR: *(boisterously)* Pull your socks up high and join a protest march! You'll show the world, and you'll see everyone's pissed off! And they'll never give up that ship!

The music stops.

PHILOSOPHR: *(compassionately)* Hey, pal. You say your car ran outta gas and the digital dashboard was hacked so you didn't know your tank was empty and the car stopped in the middle of nowhere during a big rainstorm and you can't get any reception on your phone but that's okay because you forgot to pay your bill when your reminder app stopped reminding you after an automatic firmware update and the phone service was shut off and the nearest pay phone is three miles back but you don't even know if pay phones still work and the gas station is just a mile away but you're boycotting the brand because of their unethical treatment of Indigenous women and baby seals and your girlfriend's crying because her latest selfie only got 12 likes and you start to walk toward the gas station when an 18-wheeler comes whizzing by through a large puddle and you get soaked and a raccoon comes by and steals the gas can right out of your hand and the radio announces that the president just launched nuclear weapons and you're not sure if you have enough La Croix at home to get through the apocalypse? Is that what's got you glum, chum?

Cymbals crash and a brassy rendition of "National Emblem" plays.

PHILOSOPHR: *(boisterously)* Lift your chin up and take a look at the sky! And you'll...

The PHILOSOPHR pauses as they look up to the rafters. They reach into one coat pocket and pull out a noose that they hang around their neck. They reach into the other coat pocket and pull out a bottle of poison with prominent skull-and-crossbones label and a silly straw. They start sipping noisily from the bottle as they exit the stage.

END OF SCENE. BLACK OUT.

POPPYCOCK RISING

A lighthearted look at the struggles that writers face in the modern gig economy.

<u>CAST:</u>
NAT
SID
MEL

When possible, all characters should be cast either female-identifying, non-binary, or gender-neutral

SETTING: *A busy coffeeshop, filled with writers using laptops*

NAT and SID are sitting at separate tables next to each other, typing on their laptops.

NAT: *(slams her laptop closed)* That's it! I'm done.

SID: Wow, already? You work fast.

NAT: No, no, no. I'm done. Over it. I'm fed up with this hokum!

SID: Hokum? That's strong language for a coffee shop.

NAT: Hokum. Bunk. Hogwash. *Malarkey*.

SID: What are you working on?

NAT: My client ordered horoscopes for a corporate newsletter, where the predictions are tied in with the brand and "foster office productivity".

SID: Ouch. There's a horoscope for everything now, seems like. I'm writing Back to School horoscopes with a Harry Potter theme.

NAT groans.

SID: Not a Potterhead?

NAT: I'm a writer, not an astrologer. Now, it's not enough to learn all this gobbledygook about star alignment and Mercury in retrograde, we've gotta be hip to the lingo of some cockamamie subculture they just invented yesterday.

SID: Ah, like horoscopes for Millennial Instagram influencers?

NAT: And horoscopes for Goth Yoga Enthusiasts.

SID: Horoscopes for the Civil War re-enactment society of Chattanooga.

NAT: No alignment of the stars is gonna change the outcome of that one, Bubba. None of it matters, of course. All anyone really wants to know is whether they're about to meet their soulmate or win the lottery.

SID: *(shrugs)* It's fun, like celebrity gossip or personality quizzes.

NAT: Pseudoscience hooey! Nobody even understands astrology — they just pick up the local commuter rag and imagine they're getting sage wisdom from some mystic swami in a turban instead of banal platitudes from a desperate writer in a musty bathrobe who's blithely attributing woo-woo nonsense to floating space rocks.

SID: So we give folks a bit of confidence, maybe a little nudge to snap out of the daily doldrums.

NAT: Or we're giving them a scapegoat for when things don't work out.

SID: Pessimist.

NAT: *Sagittarius.*

SID: I'm a Virgo, actually.

NAT: Oh, yeah? Here's a nice astrological forecast for you: Venus is ghosting Saturn, so sleep on your left side tonight and think twice about asking for that raise.

SID: What, no lucky lotto numbers?

NAT: We're not writing fortune cookies here.

SID: You don't believe planetary factors can influence human behaviour at all?

NAT: Weather? Yes. The environment? Absolutely. Neptune putting Orion's belt on backwards? Not so much. The planets don't deserve to be saddled with our chaos.

SID: What about the tides?

NAT: Don't give me the tides.

SID: You can't deny that the phases of the moon have some impact on your mood.

NAT: So can sunshine, humidity, and a snowstorm in May. A cherry danish can impact my day but I wouldn't devote myself to a belief system built around baked goods.

SID: Well, there's nothing wrong with trying to make people feel better about their day. You can't spell horoscope without hope.

NAT: Spare me! Alright, say we give people a little hope — "Jupiter is in conjunction with Mars in your second house today, so go ahead and take a big risk." Nobody knows what that means, but what if it inspires someone to gamble away their life savings or get divorced? Lives may be ruined over some generalized zodiac bullshit? We'd be named in so many lawsuits if we wrote under our own byline.

SID: Okay, some of the star stuff does seem farfetched. On the other hand, Astrology's been around since the 11th century; why would people practice something for centuries if there wasn't some value in it?

NAT: Slavery's been practiced for centuries. You think there's value in that?

MEL enters and approaches the cluster of tables where NAT and SID are seated.

MEL: Hi, is this the screenwriters' section?

NAT: No, the screenwriters are over by the espresso machine.

SID: This is the horoscope writers' section.

MEL: Perfect.

MEL sits down near NAT and SID, opens her laptop, starts typing.

SID: Are you an astrologer?

MEL: Amateur astrologer, professional writer.

NAT: Welcome to the club.

MEL: Misery loves company.

SID: Another non-believer?

MEL: Let's just say tabloid astrology isn't my cup of tea leaves, but it helps pay the bills.

SID: A gig's a gig. You don't have to be passionate about the subject matter as long as you can meet the word count.

MEL: Except people count on these words.

NAT and SID groan.

MEL: Sorry, did I say something wrong?

NAT: Oh, we were just in a heated debate over the purpose of horoscopes.

SID goes to the newspaper rack and grabs a newspaper. She opens the paper to the horoscopes page and shows it to MEL and NAT.

SID: Exhibit A: the standard disclaimer for every horoscope column — "For entertainment purposes only".

NAT: *(scoffs)* Some entertainment.

SID: I thought you were done anyway, Nat.

NAT: I am. Through. Finito.

MEL: *(to NAT)* You're giving it up, why?

SID: Don't get her started again.

NAT: All the effort we put into reading charts and doing deep dives into ancient zodiac history is pointless. At the end of the day, we're just writing generic advice columns and slapping a star sign on every paragraph. And readers are suckered in because it appeals to their vanity.

SID: Not that there's anything wrong with that.

MEL: This is a tough job. I haven't been at it very long but I've already gotten letters from real astrologers cursing me for tarnishing their credibility. I really try to get it right, it's just, with word counts and client demands, there's barely room to mention the celestial events that might influence our promises of good fortune and tranquility.

NAT: If only the clients would consult with "real" astrologers for their Dungeons and Dragons horoscopes.

SID: I think folks are content with vague cosmic stuff. They know some things are beyond Earthly control. That's enough, right?

MEL: *(to SID)* You don't think readers should be presented with the facts behind astrological forecasts?

NAT: Facts? Ha!

MEL: The moon is shrinking, did you know?

SID: No. Really? Who says?

MEL: NASA.

NAT: What — did a couple of astronauts take a tape measure to it while on a space walk?

SID: How is the moon shrinking — isn't it basically a giant rock?

MEL: I don't know, the article I read said it was something to do with moonquakes, but they hadn't identified the cause yet.

NAT: Ooh! "Moonquakes" would be a great title for a sci-fi romance novel.

An inspired NAT pulls out a notebook and starts making notes.

MEL: Don't you think we should find out what impact moonquakes might have on the gravitational pull and how it all influences our horoscopes?

SID: "There are more things in heaven and Earth…" Besides, that's above our pay grade.

NAT: Yeah. Next you'll be saying we should account for meteors and satellites and Chinese space garbage.

MEL: Our understanding of the universe and our relationship to space have evolved over time. And yet, astrology remains rooted in a system developed before rocket ships and telescopes. How accurate can our horoscopes be if we don't take into account how manmade objects in space might disrupt the natural order of things?

SID: Are you suggesting we overhaul an entire system of belief that's based on thousands of years of observation?

MEL: No, but there's room for revision. After thousands of years, astrologers have gotten pretty lax with their observations over the last fifty or so years.

NAT: *(sarcastically)* Thanks, NASA!

MEL: The more insight we can provide, the better people can start to understand themselves and the universe.

NAT: Look, I admire your integrity — I lost mine several sun cycles ago. Your average horoscope followers are not known for their innate curiosity. Like Sid said, they're fine with the vague cosmic rationale, especially if it validates their personal choices. And, well, the poor soul who depends on the astrological guidance in a newsletter for the vegan knitters of Northern Michigan probably deserves whatever misfortunes befall them.

MEL: Whether or not we believe in astrology, a lot of people do, and we owe it to them to present the most accurate data available. How can we be trusted otherwise?

SID: Remember a few years ago, when NASA discovered a new astrological sign — Orpheus, I think it was?

MEL: Oh, I read about that. Ophiuchus [o-FYOO-kuhs] — it's the 13th constellation in the Western zodiac, right?

SID: Something like that. Anyway, while it's technically, scientifically accurate, you don't meet anyone claiming to be "such an Ophooey-curse" because, for one, it's a weird name for a star sign and two, nobody wants to give up such a core piece of their identity, however wrong it may be. So we're stuck with the same old twelve star signs and old-fashioned horoscopes.

NAT: I remember that week! I was an Aries for a day and a half and felt like a completely different person. My ex-boyfriend said I was still a selfish bitch, but I won $5 off a lotto scratcher. Thanks, NASA!

SID: But you don't believe in this stuff.

NAT: As a Taurus, no. As an Aries, I could be more open to possibilities.

MEL: So, I should just give up.

NAT: That's the spirit!

SID: Or give in and embrace the tradition.

NAT: Don't get me started on tradition.

SID: As much as you would like to believe that your words have the power to influence, our horoscopes are nothing more than a reassuring little ritual for most folks. Life is hard, the world is on fire, the daily news is full of grief and despair. When everything feels bleak and unpredictable, we seek out comfort in the familiar. People know what they're getting with their horoscope. Even the non-believers can take a little solace in the fact that they can rely on horoscopes to deliver the same old bullshit. It helps to know that Mercury is still going into retrograde and a new moon is the best time to start a new project. For a fleeting moment, Capricorns and Cancers can imagine that there are still fortunes to be made and new romances just around the corner. We don't have to be trustworthy, we just have to be reliable. Before I started writing horoscopes, I was under contract to what turned out to be a white nationalist's travel blog. I'd much rather be writing about the age of Aquarius than the second coming of the Third Reich.

NAT: Well, when you put it that way...

MEL: So, we just keep cranking out misinformation and half-truths? I was an award-winning investigative journalist... Is this my life now — reduced to writing cheap horoscopes and product descriptions for smartphone accessories?

NAT: Until we're replaced with A.I. bots. Once those things can be trained to generate content, we're done for in any field. *(shouts across coffeeshop to unseen character)* Hey, Mike! Better get that screenplay finished before the robots come for you!

They all sit in resigned silence for a beat.

NAT: You know what, I think I'm ready to take my psychic's advice and finally finish my novel.

NAT opens her laptop and starts typing.

SID: Now?

NAT: Why not?

SID: You'll have to move over to the novelist section.

NAT: Oh. Right. Well… see you in the funny pages, ladies.

NAT takes her laptop and bag and moves to another table in the coffeeshop. MEL and SID sigh as they open their laptops and resume typing.

END OF SCENE. BLACK OUT.

About Katharine!

Katharine is the author of the best-selling *30 Failures by Age 30*, *The Curable Romantic: Advice for the Romance-Impaired*, *Slantindicular: Stories Among Other Things* and the author-illustrator of *BORIS: Robot of Leisure*.

Katharine is also an artist and graphic designer specializing in low-brow pop art inspired by 20th century popular culture. Katharine's paintings, part of her Robot of Leisure series, have been exhibited in galleries and public spaces across North America. View more of her work at thatkatharine.com.

PRODUCTION REQUEST

If your company would like to produce or perform scenes from Raspberries and Rhubarbs, please visit our website sparklingobservationalist.weebly.com/production-request.html

Complete the contact form with the following information:

- Company name
- Location (city, proposed venue)
- Performance date range
- Number of performances
- Seating capacity
- Average ticket price
- Type of group performing (professional, community, university, etc.)
- Type of performance (mainstage, black box, staged reading, festival, in-school performance, etc.)

Performance of this play may be subject to a royalty.

Please note: no part of this work can be performed or reproduced in any way without written permission from the author/publisher. No changes to dialogue, language, or characters can be made without written permission from the author.

(The author is open to consider substitutions and casting suggestions and is willing to be engaged in the production process, so please feel free to ask.)

www.ingramcontent.com/pod-product-compliance
Lightning Source LLC
Chambersburg PA
CBHW050435010526
44118CB00013B/1535